SOCIALLY INTELLIGENT SELLING

THE GROUND-BREAKING WAY TO CLOSE LESS AND WIN MORE

JAMIE SUMMERS

R∃THINK PRESS

First published in Great Britain 2017
by Rethink Press (www.rethinkpress.com)

CONTENTS

I dedicate this book to my husband.

Your inspiration runs through every page.

Life has no meaning without you.

INTRODUCTION

At the centre of every sales team you'll find one or two consistent top performers. The ones who stand out from the crowd. The ones who are admired by peers from afar. The ones who are used to people saying they're naturally good at selling. The special ones.

You'll probably have worked with people like this or know some of them in your network. They're one of a kind.

Salespeople like this are highly valued in business because:

- They consistently bring in repeat business
- They have the highest referral rate in the team
- They have the highest conversion rates in the team
- They are perfect for cultivating new sales performers
- They just "get it"

People like this stand out from the crowd for other reasons too. It isn't a coincidence that they're naturally inquisitive about other people, that they're remembered for being charismatic, that they ask great questions (and wait to hear the answers) and that they seem to be much more interesting than most people.

These people are **socially intelligent**. So, what is social intelligence?

It's a person's ability to effectively navigate and negotiate social relationships and environments.

It's this ability to interact in social situations that makes us who we are. According to psychologist Nicholas Humphrey, writing in the *Journal of American Science* in 2015, it is someone's social intelligence rather than their quantitative intelligence (their IQ) that makes them human.

But social intelligence is much more than an ability to hold down a simple conversation. In his 2006 book, *Social Intelligence: The New Science of Human Relationships*, Daniel Goleman asserts that social intelligence is made up of two things: social awareness (which includes empathy and receptiveness) and social facility (which includes connection and influence).

When social intelligent people work in sales, it's a recipe for huge success.

Gone are the days when people accepted pushy salespeople. We don't stand for that any more. Times have changed and we have changed. We've become more aware of how we feel when we interact with others. We have entered an era where we're much more likely to part with our money if someone has made us feel good. The product is almost secondary.

A saying by the wonderful author Maya Angelou forms the basis of this book:

"I've learned that people will forget what you said, people will forget what you did, but people will never forget how you made them feel."

Each of the training modules in this book is designed to ensure that you become aware of how you are making people feel. After all, that's what you'll be remembered by.

This brings me to my story.

When I was twenty-four I applied for my first sales job as an estate agent in Manchester, England. I told them straight that I was no good at sales, but if they wanted me as a receptionist then I would be perfect. To my surprise the owner offered me a sales job there and then. Fast forward a couple of years and I was headhunted to open the most prestigious estate agent that Manchester was yet to see. From that, I worked in increasingly high-profile sales roles until the ultimate job came along – teaching people how to sell at Apple Retail in London.

After spending my time working for other people I decided to capture my methodology and start sharing it with others through training. In 2013 my husband and I set up The Skills Farm, where we teach men, women and teams across the country how to be the ultimate salesperson.

The great thing about my methodology is that it's so simple. It's about learning how to be human again, how to be interested in one another, how to ask powerful questions and how to show respect by actively listening to what the other person has to say. In this book you will learn how to strip back old habits and rediscover the true salesperson in you.

You may need to read this book more than once to squeeze every last drop of value out of it. Because when you put into practice what I am teaching you, you will be astounded by the increase in your ability to sell.

The easiest way to know if you're getting it right is to examine how you feel. If it feels like you're not selling, you've cracked it.

Being able to tune into your social intelligence is the key to being an outstanding salesperson. Let me show you how...

CHAPTER 1

CASE STUDY – FUSIONTECH

Located under railway arches in a trend-setting area of South London, FusionTech has a small sales force, complete with an onsite repair shop. It specialises in retailing well-known brands of computers and sells GoPros and drones, the latest gadgets and computer accessories. They are the go-to place for the latest tech goodies. FusionTech not only survived the recession but also expanded by opening two more units. But in the last year the sales figures have been disappointing, and this is threatening the company's ambitions to open premises in Manchester. The CEO, Andrew, needs growth to fund the expansion plan but the numbers are simply not adding up. Every new and costly sales campaign the outgoing sales director, Simon, implemented proved successful for a while – but these only got FusionTech to a certain level of success. By mutual agreement, Simon was allowed to go and Adrienne was headhunted from a mobile phone company, where her sales results were outstanding.

It's been exactly two weeks since Adrienne was recruited to replace Simon at FusionTech, which opened for business in 2007. It's Monday morning and Andrew has arranged a 9am meeting with Adrienne to hear her plans to increase sales. Andrew has arrived ready to talk business. At times, he can be abrupt and terse, and he tends to dominate meetings. He responds best to facts and figures, and today it's all about the figures. He hasn't had much contact with Adrienne since she started. She's been settling into her new role and finding out what's gone wrong in the sales division. As he hands her a coffee, he looks her in the eye and says:

"FusionTech's come a long way since 2007. None of us knew what was about to happen when the market crashed. Nobody saw it coming. But I wasn't going to let that stop me. Quite the opposite, in fact. It made me more determined. As soon as I opened those doors, I began building it from nothing to where it is now, with a £6m annual turnover."

Adrienne nods. "I know. I've read articles about you in the trades. How FusionTech bucked the trend, despite all the odds; how it went from strength to strength." She flatters.

Andrew leans back in his chair. It's obvious he's proud of what he's achieved.

"That was down to me. Every quarter I set the targets for growth and every quarter we hit them. And each month our customer database grew. In year three we opened King's Cross and in year five, Shoreditch, bang on plan. But ever since then, that lot out there can't seem to sell. All I see is our competition going great guns and us stuck in the mud. So I'm assuming you're going to tell me what you're going to do about it. What's your plan?"

Adrienne has worked with several CEOs like Andrew, who are traditionally task-driven and focused on the numbers. Each CEO has proved to be a challenge, but Adrienne has a different set of leadership skills, which often bring her into conflict with the board. She is much more people-focused in her approach – she makes a point of asking questions and listening before she acts. CEOs like Andrew, in her experience, don't operate that way. The pressure they've experienced in their roles has hardened them and they've lost touch with their people skills. She opens up the company brochure she has brought with her.

"It says here that the company's vision is to be the most trusted IT and gadget retailer in the UK."

"Correct."

"But we only have fifty-five staff. Which isn't a lot if we want to cover the whole of the UK."

"Which is precisely why we need to expand – but we can't do that unless we get the sales figures up."

Andrew's tone is tetchy, which is what Adrienne expects. She presses him.

"Why Manchester in particular?"

"We considered Birmingham but it's already too competitive there. Manchester business rates are lower and we can still distribute product there easily enough. If that's where the northern powerhouse is going to be, I want us to be there too, right from the start. It's an opportunity, which is why you need to sort out our sales problem."

"When I started here, you told me we need to increase sales based on a five per cent margin if the business is going to expand."

"Correct."

"But that's not going to happen until we address the underlying issues that have created a barrier to increasing sales."

"What underlying issues?"

"We need to understand what's changed, Andrew – why they're not hitting their targets. It's pretty much the same group of guys doing the same job as they were two years ago, but they're just not achieving these new targets. We *know* they can sell, up to a limit: the figures speak for themselves, as you said. In all honesty, the sales figures aren't that bad —"

"They're still not good enough."

"Because we've reached as far as we can go, that's why. We've hit that glass ceiling."

"Oh, that old chestnut. How do you think we can smash through this glass ceiling of yours?"

"Training. When did they last have any formal sales training?"

"You'd need to ask Simon that, and since he's no longer here..."

"No need. I can answer that for you. Never."

"What? No sales training whatsoever?"

"None."

Adrienne continues. "What does the number one UK football club do the day after it wins a match? Gets back on the pitch and trains. FusionTech's problem is it won the game once but since then has never retrained the team."

"What about the sales manual? They've all got their own copies – at least Simon made sure of that."

"I don't know if you've read it recently, Andrew, but in my opinion it's outdated, not very useful and certainly won't help them hit their targets. Things have changed out there since whoever it was wrote that manual. Customers have changed. It's no wonder the sales team have got their shortcomings."

Adrienne slides a sheet of paper across the table with her summary of FusionTech's stagnant approach to sales. Andrew, impressed with her diligent research, eagerly scans it. He takes in the information quickly, nodding his understanding.

1. The sales team are "order takers" – they only respond to what the customer says they want, not to what else they might want.

2. They don't convert enough potential customers into actual customers, resulting in low conversion rates in comparison to our competitors.

3. They fail to anticipate customers' needs, so they are not proactive.

4. They aren't selling enough product to their existing customer base and aren't getting to know them or their needs.

5. They aren't consistently cross-selling the company's other products, such as add-ons and peripherals (computer cases, extended warranties, external hard drives, additional software, etc.).

6. They aren't up-selling higher-value products that the customer would benefit from, such as more powerful units for video rendering or other processes requiring bigger RAM capacities.

7. There are regular inconsistencies in team members' sales results.

After a moment, Andrew leans across the desk and says, "Okay, I get it. What's your suggestion for fixing all this?"

"I propose we invest in a short-term sales training programme."

"You mean, spend *more* money? That last sales push of Simon's cost us fifteen grand, with nothing to show for it. Complete waste."

"This isn't about a campaign. It's an investment."

"Investment in what?"

"There's a training company I've used before, The Skills Farm. Jamie Summers runs the sales training. I propose we bring him in. It's only for the short term. Believe me, I've seen extremely positive results from this before."

"What does he do that you can't?"

"Training. He'll give the team the right tools to spend more time talking with potential customers. They're good, but they lack something special – Jamie can give them that magic touch. With a bit of help from Jamie, I believe they can be some of the best in the business. And our customers won't even think of picking up the phone to another IT and gadget retailer, ever again."

"Why can't *you* just train them?"

"I'm not a trainer. Jamie uses a methodology that works really well, and he's an expert in training. Sales teams really respond to the way he operates, trust me. I can show you the results from my old company."

Adrienne passes another sheet of paper to Andrew, who grabs it and scans it from top to bottom. He nods, impressed. Adrienne presses her point:

"He really knows how to give them that edge we're looking for. I know that if we bring him in, you'll see things improve almost immediately."

"And you can definitely vouch for this chap?"

"Absolutely."

Suddenly Adrienne's tone changes. She becomes softer, yet seems more passionate. "The sales team sell products well, but they don't have good relationships with our customers. They're struggling to keep up, Andrew, and none of them really know what to do to make things better. Most of them want to – they're good people, committed to the business. Since I joined, I've made a point of talking to them and I've listened to what they have to say."

"And what *do* they have to say? Why aren't they able to hit their targets? What do they have to say about that?"

"Most of the time they blame the quality of their sales leads – usually a long list of names and numbers. They're expected to 'sell, sell, sell' without any real thinking behind that, and they can't wait for those sales campaigns to end. The problem is, they're focused on quantity, not quality. They're reactive, not *proactive*."

"And if we don't do this training?"

"I don't think we'll open in Manchester – or, at least, not in a timescale you'll be happy with. And even if we do, we'll be facing the same old problems all over again. An immediate rush of sales followed by no growth down the line. But if we show the world we're investing in expert sales training, we'll attract new talent and they'll be hungry for success. And that makes Manchester much more of a possibility."

Andrew stands up and walks over to the conference room window, with its view across the sales floor. He looks at the employees all busy at their workstations for a few moments, contemplating. After a moment, he turns to Adrienne.

"You think this is the best approach?"

"I do."

"Well, in that case, bring him in. As soon as possible. I'd like to meet this Jamie Summers."

Adrienne breathes a small sigh of relief, heads straight back to her desk and picks up the phone.

CHAPTER 2

UNDERSTANDING THE CLIENT

The initial phone call

It's been over six months since I last worked with Adrienne, so when I see her name flash up on my mobile I have an inkling this isn't going to be a personal call.

"Hi, Jamie, it's Adrienne. Do you remember me? We worked together at the beginning of the year."

"Yes, of course! How are you?"

"Good, thanks – really good."

"How's Pete?"

"He's brilliant, thank you – the wedding went well."

"That's brilliant. Congratulations!" I am genuinely pleased for her.

"And guess what? We moved from Bournemouth to London three months ago. I've got a new job, which I'd like to talk to you about."

Adrienne, originally from Hungary, speaks in a clean, crisp tone, with only a trace of her native accent detectable. She arrived in the UK five years ago, having left her role as marketing director for a small but successful mobile telecoms business in Budapest. She previously told me that she was sad to leave her home, friends and family, and her job, which she loved. She was ambitious though, and wanted to broaden her horizons by taking on a bigger role and to feel more "international". That was when she was recruited by her last company and moved from Hungary to Bournemouth. She met Pete, a software engineer, within the first month and they have been together ever since. He was born and bred on the south coast, with family all around him. I guessed that Adrienne needed to call on all her powers of persuasion to get him to uproot and move to London. That's the kind of person she is – she has an ability to fully form her argument, make a considered case for change and then recruit others to her cause to bring about that change. Obviously, that approach was working well in her private life too.

"That's great," I say. "It's a big step, moving to London. Tell me a little about your new job and how it's going."

"It's a really good move for me. Actually, I was headhunted again. It's a company called FusionTech. Andrew, the CEO, messaged me on LinkedIn. I went for the interview, we got on really well, I liked what he told me about the company and I knew it was the right opportunity."

"How did he find out about you?"

"He'd read about me in the trades and the award for the campaign I was running from Bournemouth and, well, now here I am. Of course, thanks to you for working with me on those sales training courses of yours. Without you getting my sales team into shape, I might not have been such big news."

"It was your idea to bring me in."

"I know, but I couldn't have done what you did – you're the specialist. After that, the company turned itself around. They're doing really well now."

"You weren't tempted to stay on or ask for a rise?"

"Oh, they offered me that when I told them about FusionTech. They were very generous. You know me, though, always looking for something else to get my teeth into. I've been wanting to move to London for a while, so when FusionTech offered me the job, I knew it was right. I needed a new ... challenge."

Adrienne is a motivated, career-focused individual. She's bright, breezy and professionally brusque when needed, and she's full of warmth and positivity, even when things are difficult at work. I was pleased that she still had the courage to embrace change, but I sensed a little caution in her voice when she said the word "challenge".

"And is it?" I ask, probing her to open up a little more.

"You could say that."

"Okay. Tell me a bit about what hasn't been working for them."

"Basically, they've hit a glass ceiling, turnover's flattened out and profit margins are too small. It's a bit like the last time, but things at FusionTech got a little ... how shall I say – messy – before I joined. They fired the last sales director, which is when they got in touch with me. That was two weeks ago and since then I've been finding my feet, looking at what our problems are, getting to know the business inside out. It's a really dynamic company, but it's not moving forward as much as we'd like."

"What's the company's vision?"

"Well, we're still growing, just not as quickly as Andrew would like. He wants to expand the business beyond London and he's asking me what I'm going to do about it. He wants a plan in place that gives him the money from increased sales to expand without taking on any more liabilities."

"Tell me a little more about the company and how it operates."

"The main thing I've been doing is looking at how we can improve our sales team, and I've identified several problems we need to fix."

While I take notes, Adrienne shares her thoughts on why sales are floundering. The seven issues she has listed are no surprise. I've heard them many times before.

Adrienne describes a sales team made up of order takers, who aren't converting enough leads or anticipating their customers' needs. They're missing opportunities to up-sell and cross-sell and are showing inconsistent results.

Adrienne continues. "They've been left to stagnate for too long. Their procedures are, frankly, archaic. The sales manual hasn't been updated since the business began, from what I can tell, and nobody seems to be capable of fresh thinking. That's why they let Simon go and brought me in."

All of this is crucial information about not only the sales team but also the leadership team, what they've tried to fix so far and why it hasn't worked.

I ask her, "How big is the sales team? And what are they like?"

"Really good guys, honestly – a nice bunch. We've got three managers and fifteen salespeople in total. Most of them have been with the business since it started. They've got the will to succeed but they don't yet have the skills to be as polished as they could be. There's only so much I can do, and right now I need to be spending time on planning campaigns."

It's important that I repeat back to Adrienne the key information so that I understand what the overview looks like and what the problem is.

"Let me make sure I've heard this right. The company

wants to grow more quickly than it is doing now. To do this, it needs to bump up its sales significantly. You've got fifteen salespeople and three managers. I'm hearing that there's not been much formal training, if any, that you're aware of. They have a real willingness to succeed as a team but you've identified at least seven clear problems with their selling technique."

"Exactly. Jamie, I want to bring you in. I think it's really important that you meet Andrew, but he's not totally bought in to bringing on board somebody external. He says he'll have a meeting with you, though. Are you up for it?"

"What can you tell me about him?"

"Because he's the one who's got the company to where it is today, right now he thinks all we need to do is push the sales team more. He brought me in because Simon didn't have that in him. He's not convinced we need somebody like you."

From what Adrienne is saying, I'm building a snapshot of Andrew. I'm guessing he's a little out of date with how people buy and how to use influencing techniques. Quite often, leaders like Andrew work their way up through companies, but the training they received when they started out gets left behind. As leaders, they outgrow their existing skills and need a new set of abilities. Similarly, Andrew can't understand why the sales team's abilities and revenues aren't growing. That's because they need new skills too.

Adrienne asks me directly, "When can you come in and meet with Andrew?"

We fix a date for the following Friday afternoon. I've begun to get an idea of the problems Adrienne has identified with the sales team and an impression of the leadership style in the business. But before I meet with Andrew, I need to do a little more research on him and the company.

The initial client meeting

It's 10am on Friday and I'm shown into Andrew's office. Most of the week's usual stresses and strains, deadlines, meetings and reports have been dealt with. But the working week is not yet over as he shakes my hand and formally invites me to take a seat.

Armed with the research I've carried out, I already know that FusionTech sponsors Andrew's local rugby team in South London. From the articles he is reading and posting on his LinkedIn profile I've been able to build up a picture of this savvy businessman. I can tell that he's an entrepreneur at heart, who has spent the last few years building up his company from scratch, winning peer respect. He is also community-minded. He may favour a direct style of communication but underneath it all, away from the boardroom, there is a warmth and humility about him. Since I am from North Wales, our common Celtic background will immediately help us to relate to each other. It's important that he knows I recognise all these qualities in him.

"I've been looking forward to meeting you – I'm keen to know more about the rugby club you sponsor."

Andrew asks, "Do you play rugby?"

I tell him that I've never played rugby, but I'm interested in how he came to support a rugby team and how that works. Andrew opens up about his hometown in Wales and when I mention I'm also from Wales, straight away there's direct common ground. "Oh, fantastic! Whereabouts in Wales are you from?"

I see a real change in Andrew's demeanour and openness. He expected to open the meeting with, "Right, okay. What are you going to do for us? Who else in our industry have you worked with and what results can we expect to see?" Instead, he's found himself talking about how he got into rugby, what his hometown in South Wales is like and what we have in common. I keep Andrew engaged by building on our common ground and taking a genuine interest in the things that I know interest him. It's important that I relate to Andrew authentically. While my questions come from a place of genuine curiosity, I'm using strategic relationship-building techniques. On his side, he is really enjoying talking about himself – which, of course, is what we all love doing.

But the conversation inevitably needs to turn and it's not long before Andrew wants to get down to business.

"Right, so tell me about you. Why did we bring you in here today? Adrienne's told me that she knows this great guy who she thinks can be of some help to us. Talk to me."

I establish my credibility and tell him about winning the Apple Retail Spirit of Business Award for my training in 2013 and some of my successes in coaching and mentoring their employees. He seems delighted that I've worked in the tech industry and he's a huge fan of Apple, which helps. He's keen to understand the work I did while I was there.

"So, what is it you do?"

"I teach people how to be socially intelligent when selling."

"Right, okay. How does that relate to me?"

"Well, it would help you increase your sales, which I believe is what you're looking for. That's what I teach people to do – to increase their conversion rates, to sell more, to get more of what they want through the way they communicate."

Before he can interject with another question, I jump in with "Tell me how you got to where you are today." I want to make it less about me and more about Andrew.

Andrew explains how he started the company more or less on his own in 2007, how he built it up to the success it is today, and the awards they've won. All the while I'm getting a better picture of who he is, what the company's aims and ambitions are, and where he believes it stands today. I ask him to tell me – in his own words – what he thinks the problems in the company are. I ask him, "What hasn't worked?"

"I took on this guy and he worked for me for four years. Towards the end, he just didn't have what it took."

I empathise with Andrew immediately. "You know what? I've been there too. You've hired somebody. You really hope that they've got what it takes, but they don't pull it off and you're left with it on your plate again. It doesn't feel nice."

This is followed by the slightest pause in the conversation as we both recognise that we understand each other.

Gaining Andrew's trust is important, but he also needs to know I've got what it takes to deliver the results. Because Andrew has a direct communication style, I know it's important to avoid going into too much detail about the specifics of what I do. If he wants detail, he'll ask. Instead we have a lively, high-level discussion about the seven sales problems that Adrienne has uncovered.

I spend time showing him that I fully understand the problems. I run through the solution at a high level and cover the benefits he can expect to see, and when.

I sense that Andrew is developing deeper trust in me already.

From my perspective, the meeting has gone to plan. My questions have allowed Andrew to do most of the talking, which has given me plenty of information. While the conversation was balanced, authentic, and flowed naturally, it had a clear direction.

Without Andrew knowing, I have demonstrated how my socially intelligent selling methodology works. I related to him, I explored his needs and the needs of the business, and I increased his confidence in me and my product.

I suspect it will only be a matter of days before I get the phone call.

Outlining my methodology

Next Monday, just after 9.15am, my mobile phone flashes into life and I see Adrienne's name appear again. All weekend I've been thinking about my meeting with Andrew, processing all the information I've learned about FusionTech and the problems they face with their sales.

I'm sure Adrienne has good news. I answer quickly.

"Hi, Adrienne – how are you? How was your weekend?"

"Great, thanks. Listen, I want to get straight to the point."

"About Andrew?"

"Yes."

"Okay, fire away."

I can sense from her voice that Adrienne sounds extremely upbeat, excited almost.

"We're in! Andrew's on board. You worked your magic on him. I just came out of a meeting with him – he called me in as soon as I got here. He said he enjoyed meeting you and he was really impressed with how you came across."

I smile to myself, remembering that it was Andrew who did most of the talking. "Brilliant – thanks."

Of course, it isn't magic at all. Magic is pure manipulation, because only one person knows what's really going on. Strategic relationship building is different. Andrew knew that I was there to gather information and sell myself. Both of us were fully aware of what was happening. It's the transparency of the process and the outcome that makes the clear difference between being manipulative and being influential.

Adrienne continues. "Actually, it couldn't have gone better from my point of view. Andrew said you were very warm and friendly. Andrew doesn't like warm and friendly normally, as you can imagine, but he really feels you're somebody he can do business with and he trusts your judgement. Especially after you told him you have experience working in this industry. He was impressed with your credentials and the difference you've made to other companies. He's more than happy for me to bring you in to work with our sales team. Really, there's just so much that needs fixing."

"That's great. Over the weekend I worked out a plan for how to move all this forward. We are moving ahead, aren't we?" I enquire.

"Of course we're going ahead. This is so exciting, Jamie – I can't wait to see what you're going to do for us, because this time the problem is much bigger."

"It is. That's why, based on the seven issues you've shared with me, I've prepared a high-level plan for the training course."

"I knew you'd be one step ahead," Adrienne sounds pleased.

"I'll need to know a little more about who's coming to the first course. I'd also like them to start to examine their own social intelligence in three areas – their ability to relate, their ability to discover and their ability to be credible. This will help them understand what kind of salesperson they are and where there is room for improvement."

Adrienne takes lengthy notes as she listens to me talk about the course.

"You and Andrew are going to be delighted," I continue, "because this is where you're going to see an increase in not only the volume of sales but also enhanced sales. Your sales team will learn how to be naturally curious about their customers, build deeper relationships and bring their own product knowledge into play in a way that engages the customer and has them calling back for more."

"That sounds really interesting. I already know which members of the team are going to embrace this."

"Well, it's not going to be an easy ride for them. They'll be learning a new set of skills and having to make quite a shift in their mindset."

"Hmm. Some of the participants I have in mind for the first session have been here since the beginning. One in particular might be quite stuck in his ways."

"That's not a problem. I expect that kind of reaction, and I'm used to it. After all, they won't have been trained in this way before. And when the penny drops, they'll all start to see results."

"That's exactly what they need," Adrienne agrees. "So what are our next steps?"

"I'd like to meet up with you and Andrew again briefly so that I can take you through my plans at a high level."

"Perfect. How about Wednesday – say, 11am? Come to the office. I'll book us a meeting room."

"Wednesday works for me."

*****

A couple of days later, Adrienne and I are chatting over a coffee in one of FusionTech's meeting rooms waiting for Andrew to arrive. She exudes a sense of eager anticipation about what exactly I will propose as a plan of action. She knows that I have arrived well prepared and that everything I'm about to present is based on my experience and expertise in sales training.

At ten past eleven the meeting room door swings open and Andrew breezes in carrying a cup of coffee. "Apologies. My previous meeting overran." He sits down, looks up at me and smiles warmly. "Nice to see you again Jamie." Then his smile drops. "Listen, I've only got ten minutes, what have you got?"

I immediately get down to business. "In my experience, most organisations have similar problems in sales and they usually relate to the seven issues you listed in our last meeting. What you may find useful is a brief overview of how my methodology will tackle the problems you have here at FusionTech."

I draw Adrienne and Andrew a simple diagram. Visualising my thinking in this way is an effective, immediate and dynamic technique that helps clients understand my process and link their problems to my solution.

I draw the following diagram:

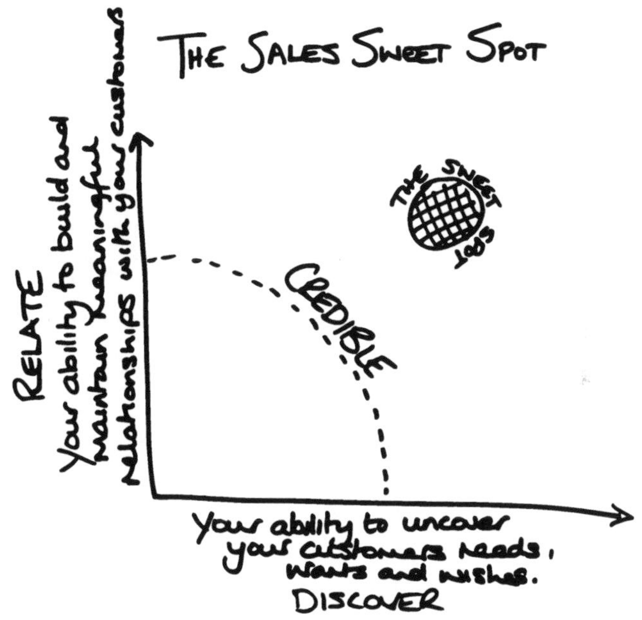

"Let's start with **relate**," I say. "In other words, how well do your sales teams build *relationships* with their customers?

"Research in social neuroscience shows that generally, people respond more positively to someone who comes across as trustworthy and relatable *before* they come across as knowledgeable and credible."

"So quickly building rapport with your customers is

essential?" Adrienne responds.

"Exactly. When I meet my customers for the first time, I quickly find and build common ground and spend a while taking an interest in the things that are interesting to them."

Andrew looks up at me. "I wondered why you didn't start by impressing me with how much success you've had." He smiles.

"I did, eventually. But that came after I had built rapport."

Andrew nods. A penny has dropped.

"The more your sales team can build and maintain non-superficial relationships with their customers, the closer they'll be to selling more and having more enhanced sales."

"Go on." Andrew was keen to hear more.

"Next is **discover**. How much do your sales team *explore* with your customers?

A good investigator will ask questions to uncover their customer's needs, wants and wishes. This often leads to a customer revealing needs they didn't even know they had. Of course, this can't be done without impeccable listening skills and an ability to ask intelligent, probing questions. The more your sales team ask and listen, the more they'll discover and the closer they'll be to becoming socially intelligent at selling."

"Yes, and being relatable makes it easier to discover more," Adrienne states.

"That's right." I nod.

"Go on." Andrew checks his watch.

"Have you still got time?" I enquire.

"Yes. Yes. Keep going." Andrew waves his hand as if to say, keep drawing.

"The third factor we'll cover on the training course is **credible**. How credible are your sales teams?"

"I don't think they'll have any problems. They know our product range well," Adrienne offers.

"That's good, but this isn't just about them knowing what they're talking about. Of course, their customers need to think that – but on its own, even with good discovery, knowing a lot about your product or service isn't enough. Let me illustrate."

I explain how one of the world's largest IT organisations made this mistake. Each quarter their win/loss reports showed an alarming trend: their credibility wasn't winning them enough work.

Time and time again, clients gave stark feedback: "Clearly you know your stuff, but it just doesn't *feel* like we can work with you."

After months of discovery, preparing and pitching for large pieces of work, the company found that their clients preferred to work with their competitors, who the clients considered were more relatable.

Being high on the scale of credible, and even discover, but low on the scale of relate was costing them millions in lost opportunities.

Both Andrew and Adrienne are captivated.

Then I ask them a powerful question. "Can you identify where your sales team sit on the diagram?"

Adrienne studies the drawing and starts to hazard a guess as to who sits where on the chart. She quickly realises that there aren't many members of her sales team sitting in the sales sweet spot.

"I'd be surprised if there were," I confirm.

"Do you use this diagram on the course?" Andrew is curious.

"To start with, yes. Then I use a similar one with more detail. Shall I show you?"

Andrew checks his watch again. "Draw!"

I quickly sketch a similar diagram, but this time I add a grid with four quadrants.

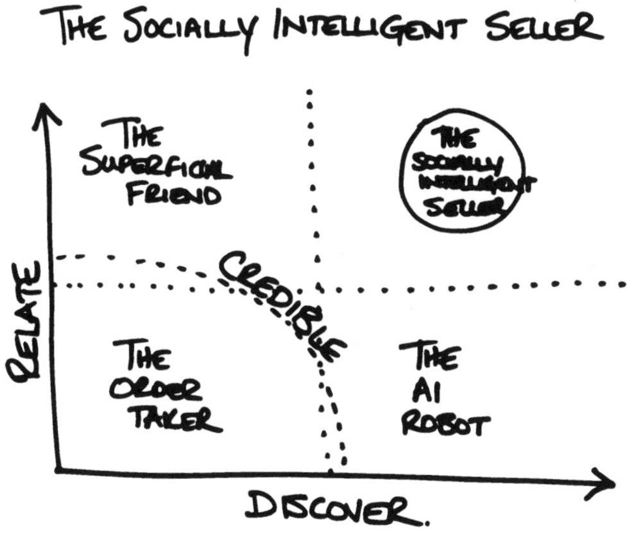

"Let me take you through it.

"Low discover and low relate is what I call the **order taker**.

"This is the salesperson who processes sales like they're orders. They ask few questions and often only give the customer what they ask for. Along the way, they do little to build the relationship and they don't gain a clear understanding of their customer's needs, wants or wishes."

Adrienne is already thinking that she has too many order takers in the team but doesn't feel comfortable to say who just yet.

"High discover and low relate is the **AI robot**. By AI, I mean artificial intelligence.

"This is the salesperson who can sound a bit artificial or robotic and can usually be found asking generic questions from a set list. They tend not to question, probe or listen, not to any meaningful level. They do achieve some sales success, but clients don't warm to them. Organisations with this type of sales team have a lower returning customer base than they could have.

"Low discover and high relate is what I call the **superficial friend**.

"This is the friendly salesperson. Unfortunately, it's all rather superficial because they don't take time to explore the customer's needs, wants and wishes comprehensively. Customers come away thinking how nice the salesperson was, but the salesperson misses opportunities to sell more and in doing so costs their organisation a great deal."

Adrienne instantly thinks of one of the members of the sales team, Ros. Could she be a culprit?

"High discover and high relate is, of course, the socially intelligent seller.

"This is the salesperson who is consistently in the sales sweet spot. They purposely take time to get to know their customer by being relatable, but they also spend time exploring and gathering as much relevant information as possible. This gives them more selling opportunities and the chance to up-sell and cross-sell on each opportunity. They often leave customers feeling that they've just received first-class service.

"A dynamic knowledge of your products and their benefits – the skill of linking a product or service to a customer's needs – is the final ingredient."

I look up at Andrew, hoping he has followed my brief explanation. I wasn't disappointed.

"My goodness, Jamie!" Andrew smiles and stands up, heading towards the door. "I have to move on to my next meeting now, but I like this a lot." He looks over at Adrienne. "I'll leave this in your capable hands," then back to me, "good luck with the training." The door closes behind.

Adrienne beams, "Jamie, this is going to be amazing. You nailed it last time and I know you're going to nail it this time. I just need to find the most receptive participants for the first workshop."

"Don't worry about that. It's the people who seem resistant at first who often progress the most."

"Okay, leave it with me. I'll select the initial group and pin down a date that suits everybody. I'll also sort out a contract for you."

"And I'll start preparing the course."

"This is so exciting – I can't wait for you to start!"

CHAPTER 3

THE WORKSHOP – DAY ONE

Two weeks later, I'm ready for day one of my sales training workshops with FusionTech. I'm the first to admit that the night before helping a new client, I'm always a little restless, partly because I'm excited to meet the team and partly because I'm itching to begin my work in earnest. Because of my vast experience in the training room and an uncanny knack of reading people, I'm not at all fazed by the thought that soon I'll be facing a group of challenging salespeople, all with individual needs, strengths and weaknesses. In that regard, every workshop is different.

What makes the first encounter with this new team easier is that Adrienne will have briefed them already. Under my instructions, she will have got them thinking about how relatable they are, how much they discover and how credible they are. She will also have asked them what they would like to get out of the workshop.

I've already identified three main objectives I'd like to meet to fulfil my commitment to FusionTech.

Objective 1: To impact the business

Ultimately, Andrew needs to see results. With FusionTech, the stakes are higher for me than working with a multinational brand because so much more rides on the outcome of the training – ultimately, FusionTech expanding outside London.

The outcome of the sales team going through my training is that they will have a new way of selling. They can implement the training quickly, so once it is fully rolled out it will give Andrew and Adrienne the five per cent increase in margin that they are looking for.

Objective 2: To impact learning

By the end of the training, through developing their social intelligence the sales team will have learned how to:

1. Consult with customers rather than just take orders
2. Convert more potential customers
3. Anticipate customers' needs
4. Sell more to existing customers
5. Cross-sell
6. Up-sell
7. Use a framework to make sales results more consistent across the team

After the workshop, I'll teach this new way of thinking to the whole of the sales force. By the end of the training, they will know how to overcome the seven problems that Adrienne highlighted in her training needs analysis by being socially intelligent at selling, and they'll all be able to apply their new skills immediately.

Before the workshop has started I'm already thinking about how FusionTech can maintain this new way of working when I'm no longer around to help them do it.

I'm going to teach the team about **fear-free feedback**, one of the most powerful development tools, which we all carry within us yet rarely use. It is important that the participants help one another to continue this development once they are all back at their desks.

Objective 3: To give the participants what they need

In my experience, this is one of the areas where other sales-skills trainers fall short. There are four considerations where participants are concerned.

1. Do they like the trainer?
2. Do they want to be there?
3. Are they getting involved?
4. Are they getting what they need?

It is important that the participants like the trainer. To help with this, my approach is informal. I like to make it known that I don't take myself too seriously, even though I take my work seriously.

There's a big difference between participants who choose to go on a workshop and those who are told they have to attend. At FusionTech the group have been told to attend – this will put up barriers in their minds before they even step into the room. I'm going to have to get buy-in for my methodology as quickly as I can.

Keeping the participants engaged throughout the two days is one of the challenges I will face as a facilitator. This is where I use the skill of keeping one eye on every response in the group while keeping the other eye on the content. Everything needs to build and come together at the right time. Dropping the ball is not an option.

The course I've designed for the sales team takes place over two full days. It requires full commitment from the business to take key salespeople out of their work environment for this period, which Andrew has agreed in advance. Typically, running the course over two days allows the following to happen:

1. The participants are more able to disconnect from work distractions, so they absorb more of the workshop content.

2. The learning aspects take root overnight and can be built on during day two.

3. It provides enough time to get past any resistance in participants.

It's 8am at FusionTech's head office and I've arrived early. I'm greeted excitedly by Adrienne, who shows me straight into the room set aside for the training. I'm quick to set up, unpacking the participant workbooks and marker pens, making sure that everyone will get a good view of the flip chart. What's unusual about the way I train is that I never use slides. Flip charts are much more flexible and it's easier to annotate them when bringing out ideas from the participants. The flasks of tea and coffee are ready and waiting and now, so am I.

I now know that I'll be training six members of the team. They represent a cross-section of the department in the three sales areas where the business meets its customer base:

1. Telesales
2. Counter sales
3. Sales meetings with clients

Welcome, introductions and objectives

It's 9.15am and the participants begin to show up for the 9.30am start. The six who have been selected work in three areas of the sales team. There are Carl and Ros in telesales, Steve and Zoë, who sell over the counter, and Naomi and Peter, who go out and sell face to face. I keep the atmosphere light and informal as they chat over their coffee, sharing jokes and stories. I use this an opportunity to establish a rapport before the training session begins. This is always a challenge on the first day of training a diverse group of salespeople.

"Before we begin," asks Steve, "is this training meant to be replacing the sales manual we all have, or supplementing it?"

"I hope it replaces it," Ros jumps in. "Since the day I got mine, it's just been sitting under my desk collecting dust."

"All will be revealed." I smile, adding a little mystery to the proceedings before they've even begun.

Once they have finished their coffees, I hand them each a workbook, open my flip chart and formally welcome them to the training. I begin by briefly introducing myself and outlining what brings them all together this morning:

"As you all know, this company has big plans. It's identified an exciting opportunity to grow by expanding into Manchester but to achieve this, it needs you, its sales team, to pioneer a new way of selling that's going to raise the finances for this move. It's something that's going to make you all visible to your management and to your potential customers. Andrew and Adrienne know they've got the right people in place, so my job is to unlock something that you probably already have. And it's something that you'll never find in a sales manual."

"It says here," interrupts Naomi as she flicks through the participant booklet, "that this course is based on your research and experience over fifteen years of selling. What exactly are you going to be teaching us?"

"Well, when I moved into sales in my mid-twenties I found that it was a skill that came naturally to me. My sales career went from strength to strength. I was often a top performer, sometimes within weeks of joining a sales team.

"What I couldn't understand was that although I worked with some incredibly intelligent people, they weren't excellent at sales. That fascinated me. The more I researched, the more I understood that it was my social intelligence that made me stand out from the crowd, not my intellect.

"I thought that if I could harness my social intelligence, anyone could. So I took the principles and concepts that I was using and formulated my own models from them. I designed this training course to teach other sales professionals how to become socially intelligent sellers.

"That means that you get to learn the same skills. Does that sound like something that would be useful for you?"

"Yes, please!" they all answer at once.

After a brief round of introductions I turn the group's attention to a gap analysis that I have drawn on the flip chart. It's important for me to gauge at the beginning of the workshop where the participants see themselves in terms of their skills and abilities. I ask them to plot themselves on the chart by answering the following questions:

1. How well do you relate to your customer?
2. How much do you discover about your customer's needs, wants and wishes?

The group write their names on sticky labels, stand up and move over to the flip chart to plot themselves on the grid.

"You're always chatting away to your customers," Carl says to Ros, "so in terms of your relatability, you're off the scale."

The group chuckle at Carl's observation.

Ros replies, "I do love my customers, but sometimes we chat away and then they end the call without even placing an order."

Ros plots herself as highly relatable but low on discovery.

Next, Carl steps forward to place his mark on the chart. He notices that he has placed himself opposite to Ros – high on discovery but low on relatability.

Zoë places her sticky label near Carl's and Naomi follows suit, but slightly higher in terms of relatability.

Peter plays it safe and places his in the middle. Lastly, Steve steps forward.

"I was one of Andrew's original team, so I'm really just here for a refresher. I think I'm already quite good at discovering customers' needs and I've always been good at making friends, so I'm going to put my mark here." He places his sticky label high on the relatable scale and high on the discovery scale.

Naomi sniggers.

Steve spins round. "What?"

"Come on," Naomi says, "there's always room for improvement."

"I know," Steve is a touch defensive. "But that's where I believe I am right now."

The group settle back into their seats.

I leave the gap analysis on the wall without referring to where the team have plotted themselves. I'll come back to this at the end of the course and invite them to reposition themselves once they have learned my sales methodology.

Fear-free feedback

With stage one of the gap analysis complete, I show another flip chart with the heading **fear-free feedback**.

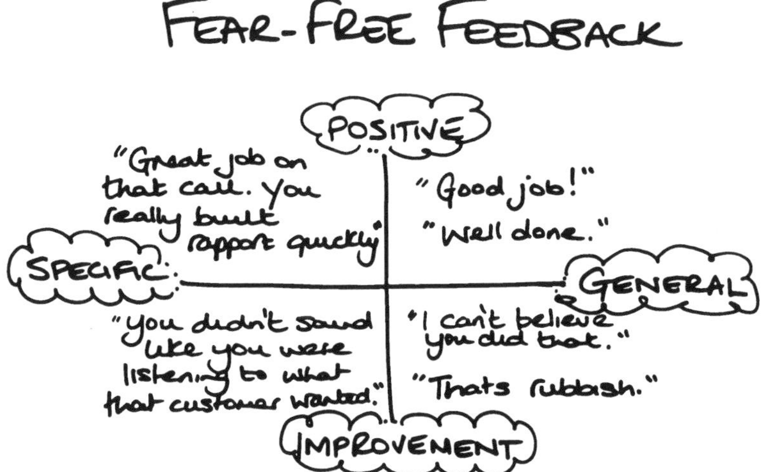

I give the group specific guidance on how they can give constructive feedback to each other throughout the course.

"I'd like you all to commit to giving fear-free feedback to someone in this room at least once today. In fact, you can give me feedback any time you like," I offer. "It's a supportive skill to get into the habit of using."

The group nod in agreement. I have experienced this vague, silent agreement before – I know they'll need a few encouraging nudges along the way before they get the hang of it.

I decide to move on. "Right, let's put a framework around what we're trying to achieve on this course."

The sales sweet spot

I turn to a new sheet of paper on the flip chart and reveal a diagram I have drawn in advance. It's the 'relate, discover, credible' chart that had won over Andrew a couple of weeks ago, when I explained my sales training methodology.

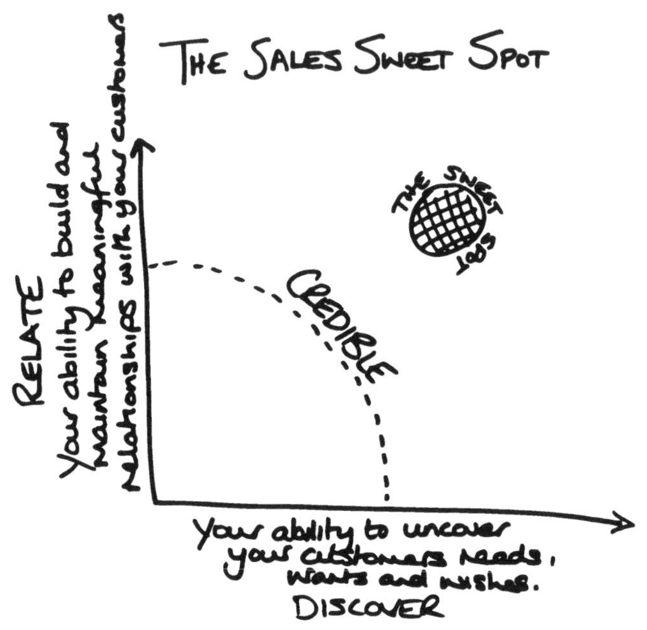

I continue, "Everything you were discussing around your gap analysis is summed up in this simple chart.

"Ros, you told us you were looking to build your confidence in discovering your customers' needs.

"Peter, you mentioned you wished you were better at building stronger relationships with your clients in the field and Zoë, you said you wanted to find out how you can be more relatable.

"Everything you've said, to a greater or lesser degree, points to this circle here – the sales sweet spot.

"Now just imagine we want that spot to grow. If you increased your ability to do these three things," I point to the words relate, discover and credible, "you'd be selling more and this sales sweet spot would be a bigger circle. That, in essence, is why we are here."

I notice the group taking notes in their booklets as I speak.

"The next two days are going to be about becoming more relatable to your customers, learning to be more naturally curious so you discover more, and knowing when to bring in your credibility, which is all the great product knowledge you've learned over the years."

Steve looks a little surprised – this is not at all what he was expecting from this sales training, and he's suddenly looking more engaged than he has done all morning. He interrupts me:

"I already do discovery. What more can I do?"

"That's what we're going to find out over the next couple of days, Steve. I'll be reinforcing some of those things you already do and you'll have the opportunity to fine-tune your existing skills, but I'll be adding new things into the mix."

"Great – if that's the case, I'm all ears."

But Naomi still seems a little uncomfortable. "I'm really confident already. I have no problems in speaking to people."

"You're absolutely right, Naomi, and you know what? Over the next couple of days, the rest of the group here will probably be looking to you to give them some pointers when it comes to confidence."

Naomi smiles.

"But I don't just teach relatability, credibility or discovery on its own. What I'm doing here is introducing to you a whole new way of selling. These three skills don't work well in isolation when it comes to sales turnover. If we focus on just one, the sweet spot will stay small – and we want it to get bigger. We can make it do that if we understand how all three skills can work together."

"So if we aren't fully relating to our customers, discovering what they need, and coming across as credible, then we aren't maximising our sales potential?" asks Carl.

"You've got it. But let's take this one level deeper." I turn the next flip-chart page and show them the socially intelligent seller model.

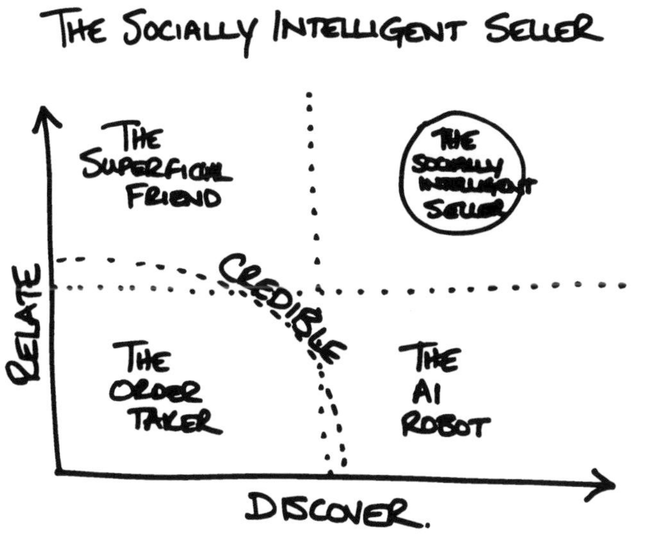

"Using the same scale – relate, discover and credible – we can now see that someone who is low on discovery and low on relating is called an **order taker**."

Everyone in the group has stopped taking notes now and is watching me and the flip chart, eager to see where I am going with this.

"Who here processes sales like they're orders? Who sells like they're a waiter taking orders in a restaurant?"

There is silence in the room while I wait for a response. For a few moments I wonder if I am pushing them to expose their weaknesses too quickly, but I am surprised when Peter puts his hand up.

"To be honest, I don't think I'd describe myself as an order taker – but I do just sell what the customer says they want. So what does this mean?"

"It means that you have an amazing opportunity here, Peter. You'll need to work hard to build relationships with your customers to gain their trust. You'll also need to learn how to do more discovery with your customers – so you can get a clearer understanding of their needs, wants and wishes."

Peter smiles and starts taking notes in his booklet.

"High discover and low relate is what I call the **AI robot**," I continue.

"Oh goodness, that's me!" Zoë pipes up.

"And me," admits Carl.

"Then to your customers, you probably sound a bit artificial or robotic. You'll be most comfortable asking generic questions from a set list."

"I am," Zoë confirms.

"You use a script?" Carl quizzes.

"Not so much a script. More a set of questions that I have in my head."

"Zoë, you're right," I acknowledge. "In my experience, you will be asking questions, but I bet you avoid probing deeper. You listen, but then ask the next question listed in your head. That means you aren't really listening at a meaningful level."

"But we're successful salespeople," challenges Carl.

"Right. But clients aren't warming to you. Your opportunity here is to be more relatable so you can dramatically increase your returning customer base."

Zoë and Carl nod. It's like I'm inside their heads. They look down at their booklets and start to take notes.

"Next we have low discover and high relate. This is the **superficial friend**." I turn to the group. "Does this describe anyone here?"

Ros is nodding. "Yes. Yes – it's me."

"And me, to a certain extent," adds Naomi.

"Then I bet your customers feel that you're approachable and friendly."

"Isn't that what we should be?" Ros asks.

"Yes, but unfortunately you tend to be rather superficial because you aren't taking time to explore the customer's needs, wants and wishes enough."

"We don't have time for that," Naomi defends.

"If that's the case then your customers are coming away thinking how nice you are. But in terms of sales, you're missing a trick. You're letting opportunities to sell slip through your friendly fingers. How much is that costing FusionTech?"

Ros is already writing in her booklet. Naomi looks me square in the eyes and for a moment I think she is going to challenge my directness. Then a penny seems to drop.

She nods and starts writing.

"Finally we have high discover and high relate – the **socially intelligent seller**. Is anyone here already selling in this way?"

Steve, the only one who hasn't openly admitted to being in any of the other quadrants, stays silent.

"This is the salesperson who consistently performs in the sales sweet spot," I explain. "They purposely take their time to get to know their customer by being relatable, but they also spend time exploring and gathering as much relevant information as possible. This gives them more selling opportunities and the chance to up-sell and cross-sell on each opportunity. They often leave a customer feeling like they've just received the best possible service."

I point to the word **credible** on the chart.

"The ability to relate and discover, along with a dynamic knowledge of your products and their benefits – the skill of linking a product or service to a customer's needs – is the final ingredient."

"Give me a moment." Steve stands up and moves towards the door.

For a second, I think that he is walking out, but Steve stops by the gap analysis and moves his sticky note down to where Peter has placed his. In the middle.

"As you've described it," he turns to me, "I think I need to be more relatable and discover more. And what you were saying then, about up-selling and cross-selling and linking products to customers – well, I don't do that either, not as much as I should."

"I'm really proud of you, Steve." I put my hand on Steve's shoulder. "It takes guts to admit you have weaknesses, especially with as much sales experience as you have."

I leave these thoughts with them while they take a fifteen-minute break. Having started the day with a combination of enthusiasm and indifference, there is now a collective sense of curiosity in the group about where this process might be leading. One of the first things to have happened is that these once disparate salespeople have begun to talk to one another as a team. They may not be aware of it just yet, but a major, positive shift in their cultural practice is happening.

Mapping the customer journey

After the break, I resume with a question to the whole group: “Who here can tell me how their customers are feeling before they part with their money?”

They all look nonplussed; it’s clear that they don’t have much idea about what I mean.

“What I want you to consider now is mapping your own customer journey.”

Ros speaks up. “I’m sorry, Jamie. I’m not sure what you mean.”

“Don’t worry, that’s why I want to show you how this works. Let’s explore, right from the beginning, how your customer is feeling after each touchpoint with FusionTech. By touchpoint, I mean an interaction with your company. Now, at least one touchpoint a customer has with this company is when they speak with you, but that’s not the whole picture. Let’s look at this from the moment they’re thinking of buying a GoPro. What’s the first thing they’ll do before calling you?”

“They might search for it on the internet,” says Carl.

“Or read one of our blogs,” adds Peter.

"Exactly," I reply. "So, they then pick up the phone and dial the FusionTech sales number. Then what happens?"

"They could end up speaking with me," says Ros, beaming.

"They might – but how often does a customer have to wait on hold before they actually get to speak with you? Do you ever stop to think that your customer has been on an emotional journey and that they'll continue on that journey until after their interaction with the company is finished?"

Ros almost squeals, "Oh my God – I never thought about it like that before. I can see how this is going to be very useful."

I continue, "Zoë's customer might have been online and even read the same blog as Ros's phone customers, but their journey is completely different. This time, they're passing the store and they decide to drop in. Maybe Zoë's busy with another customer and there's a queue for help. They wait for quite a while before they get to speak to Zoë. Now, wouldn't it be useful at this point if Zoë was more aware of what had happened to the customer before she interacted with them? Would she have altered the way she connected with the customer if she knew they'd been waiting to speak to her?"

The group nod in agreement, and I set them off with mapping their own customer journey.

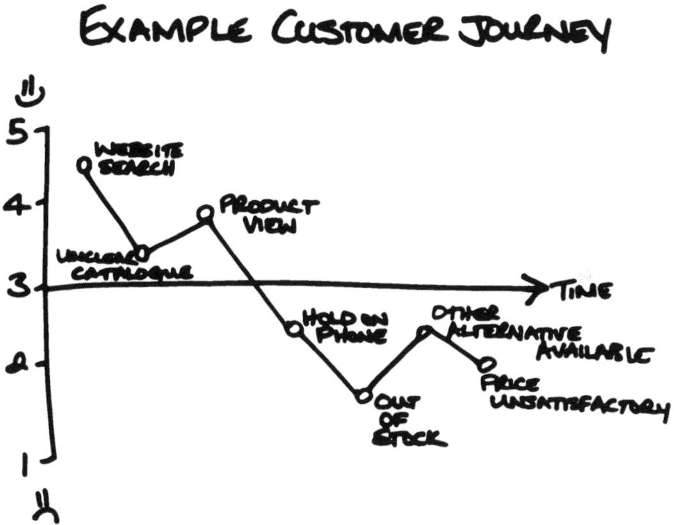

Once the group has completed their exercise, I help them dissect what it all means. What they take away from this exercise is that the outcome of a customer journey is determined by the customer's most recent interaction with the company and their deepest low. The team are surprised that their customers experience such highs and lows during their time simply looking for a product. They now start to capture in their workbooks where they have opportunities to empathise with their customer, which shows them where they can have more influence.

Carl pipes up, "I've always been so focused on what I do that I've never stopped for a second to think about how a customer is feeling before they interact with me and how much this can affect what they buy."

"I agree," nods Zoë. "I think I have a lot of opportunity to understand more about my customers, too."

"Great. The customer journey shows that every decision a customer makes is emotionally driven. The question is, how do you interact with that person when they are emotional?" I ask.

"Hang on a minute," Naomi is looking frustrated again. "If something's out of stock or there aren't enough people to answer the phones, how's any of that our fault? We can't sell what we haven't got or answer the phones any quicker."

I'm pleased that this question has cropped up. "I agree, but what you need to do is stop that customer turning from a fan of the business into a detractor."

Turning detractors into promoters

"You've all mapped your own customer journey and reflected on how seeing FusionTech through the eyes of your customers has been very revealing.

"This means that every time a customer feels less than positive, they are potential **detractors** – they will not speak favourably about FusionTech to their friends, colleagues or relatives."

Carl adds, "If one of my customers has been hanging on the line for ages before I can connect and they feel negative about this, to get them back into the positive bit I just say 'sorry' before they kick off."

"Okay," I nod. "What else could you do?"

"You could show some empathy," Naomi suggests.

Ros picks this up quickly. "You mean, something like, 'I appreciate it's frustrating, waiting in a queue. I don't like waiting myself, so let me get you sorted as quickly as possible.'"

"Great. What about if a product isn't in stock?" I ask.

Zoë jumps in with, "Could we look at some alternative products for you, Mrs so-and-so?"

Peter adds, "Or, 'Can I have this delivered direct to you?'"

Suddenly the sales team is thinking on its feet, and they start putting together a list of sentences and phrases that they can use to turn unhappy people into happy people. I'm delighted. It's such a simple exercise, but it's incredibly effective.

"You see, you don't need to say 'sorry' to turn your customer around – but show some genuine empathy and communicate with conviction."

I sum up, "Companies that take relational sales seriously work hard to continually improve their customer journey.

"What's interesting is that often, when a customer's looking forward to something, like buying a GoPro for a holiday, anything negative in the buying experience is amplified. This is called **high anticipation mindset**. It enhances how your customers are feeling – it makes the highs higher and the lows lower.

"A heightened negative emotion can often be reduced if you use empathy, build rapport, relate, and communicate with impact earlier in the customer journey."

The relationship rope

I notice that there is a tangible energy to the team's discussions. They are already buzzing about the opportunities to be more relatable with their customers and discover more about their needs.

I get their attention. "What I've asked you to think about so far today creates part of the whole picture when it comes to selling.

"This isn't about making more calls or visiting more clients to boost your sales volume. It's about getting the most out of your interaction with your clients. That leads them to buy more, or more expensive products, but tailored to their needs.

"I want your customers to come back to you again and again because they trust you, because they trust the company and because they like you. And for them to like you, you need to establish rapport with them. Which brings me to the **relationship rope**.

“I want you to imagine that the first interaction you have with your customer becomes the first strand of your relationship rope with them. It wouldn’t take much to go wrong for that thread to snap.

“A socially intelligent seller consciously builds deeper, more meaningful relationships with their customers. In other words, they continually add strands, so that thread becomes a string and then eventually a rope.

“In a moment I will share how you can add strands to that rope to make it stronger. Strong enough to withstand problems you may face, like not having the right stock or delivery times not suiting your customer. The thicker the rope, the more likely it is that your customer will forgive you when things go wrong and the more likely they are to come back next time they want to buy.

“Right now, if you tell a customer who’s been hanging on the phone or waiting in a queue that you don’t have what they’re looking for in stock, what happens?”

“They end the call and go somewhere else.”

"They get a little annoyed."

"They say they've wasted their time hanging on."

"What if," I ask, "you'd managed to build rapport with them during your interaction but things still went wrong and that product wasn't in stock?"

"They might not be as quick to drop us and go somewhere else," Steve replies.

"Exactly. If the customer feels you've had a meaningful conversation with them, you would've gradually created a string or even a rope strong enough to keep them connected to you."

"So," Carl clarifies, "from all the little individual strands you've given them, that could keep them as a customer, even when things go wrong."

"Right. When a customer experiences a bump or two during their journey, they're still disappointed. But if they have more rapport with you, they're more likely to be forgiving."

I give the group an exercise that explores different ways that they can add strands to their relationship ropes. They identify some excellent ways to quickly and easily strengthen customer relationships, but there is a little more depth yet to explore.

Warmth versus strength

I share with the group some research that underpins my sales training methodology. It's not a concept that the sales team will be consciously familiar with, but I find it's useful to introduce the theory because it helps to get them thinking about their whole approach to their customers. This has a huge impact on what their customers think of them – and, ultimately, influences customers' purchasing decisions. For now, I want to place the idea in front of them:

"Your customers make decisions about you in two simple ways," I begin. "One: do they like you? Are you relatable? Are you warm? And two: do you know what you're talking about? Are you credible? Are you strong?"

The group are taking notes as I speak.

"Warmth and strength are *both* vital elements of rapport – and both lead to trust, which is essential for any salesperson. But I want you to have a discussion between the six of you and answer this question. Which comes first, warmth or strength? And why?"

The group start a five-minute discussion, and quickly turn to me with a decision.

"We think warmth." Ros is the spokesperson.

"You're right. Warmth comes first. But why?"

Carl continues, "We think that people need to feel safe with you before they'll stick around to hear more about your expertise and knowhow."

"Perfect." I smile.

"But not everyone wants to chat for ages before buying a product," Steve adds.

"You're right, Steve. Later, when we look at communication styles, we'll see that some people aren't into building rapport – they want to get straight down to business. So, with these people warmth can be established quickly, within a sentence or two, and then developed later if necessary."

Steve nods, happy that his contribution wasn't shot down in flames.

"So building warm rapport before showing strong product expertise is another strand in your relationship rope. Your customers need to buy into you, before they buy into your product. Let's have a look at some other ways to strengthen your relationship ropes."

Finding common ground and taking a strategic interest

Building on the previous discussion, I expand on the relationship rope concept by introducing four ways to find and build common ground with a customer. They are part of the toolkit that will help the sales team show warmth before they show their strength. I turn to the flip chart and ask the group to imagine that their customer wants a GoPro to take on holiday to the Greek islands.

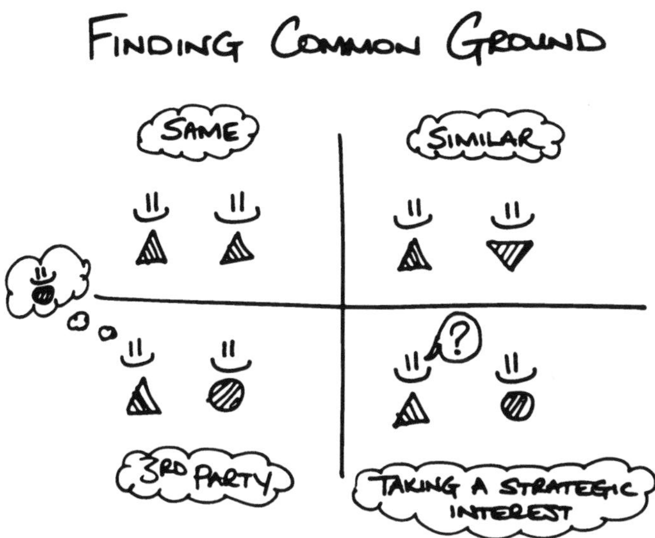

"How you could find common ground in that conversation?" I enquire.

Naomi starts them off. "Oh, Greece! Wonderful. I went last year – what's your favourite island?"

"Nice. That's **same** common ground. What about **similar** common ground?" I probe deeper.

This time Zoë contributes. "Ah, you're off to Greece. I love the Mediterranean. I went to Spain last year – which island would you recommend in Greece?"

"You're on fire. Okay, how about **third-party** common ground? This is where you don't have any same or similar common ground with the customer but you know somebody who does. This still strengthens your relationship and adds another strand to your relationship rope."

"Easy," chirps Peter. "Oh, my friend Fred runs boat excursions on one of the islands out there. Which one have you stayed on?"

"Good. How could you take that further?"

The group think for a few moments, but no one can come up with an answer.

"How about," I help them, "'Let me give you Fred's email address – he runs an amazing boating company across the Greek islands and I'm sure he can get you cheap tickets.' This connection deepens your trust and relationship with the customer."

The group nod. It's dawning on them how powerful finding and building common ground can be.

"What about this last drawing here? **Taking a strategic interest**. What's that?"

"Is it where you ask questions?" Steve enquires.

"Yes. It comes into play when you don't have any common ground. In this case, when you don't know anything about the Greek islands. You show warmth with the customer by taking an interest. What could you ask them?"

"I've never been to the Greek islands. Why are you going there?" Naomi suggests.

"Spot on. The objective behind finding common ground or taking a strategic interest is to engage your potential customer so that they feel warmth towards you.

"Holding a brief but authentic, warm conversation with your customer will help them feel you've taken an interest in them, whether you have a common interest or not.

"The fact that you've listened to and engaged with them will help the sales process to operate on a different level from 'I've come in for a GoPro.' 'Yes, we've got one for £299. Would you like it?'"

The group laugh.

"Best if all, it gives you information. It means you can use that knowledge later when up-selling or cross-selling.

"Warmth and relationship building add extra strands to the relationship rope you've created, strengthening it further. This moves you one step closer to becoming socially intelligent at selling."

In pairs, the group begin an exercise on taking a strategic interest. The exercise shows them how effective it can be to simply listen, ask questions and take a genuine interest in what the other person is interested in.

They take copious notes in their booklets as I wrap up the morning and we break for lunch.

I am conscious that the group have received a lot of information over the past three hours. They already have new approaches to use with their customers and they leave for lunch deep in thought about their past sales performance and their newly discovered potential.

I am also relieved to notice that indifference has turned to curious interest, enthusiasm has been met with considered thinking, resistance is reducing and acceptance is growing.

After lunch, things get personal.

The personal power model

As the group come back into the room I run through a quick recap to focus the team on what they have just covered.

"In this next session we're going to look at how you can become even more relatable by focusing on your personal authority and charisma."

I open the flip chart, which shows the **personal power model** represented by the personal power triangle. The purpose of this afternoon's session is to facilitate a discussion with the group so that the key learning messages are drawn out of them, not imposed on them. This technique allows the workshop participants to "own"

the learning. It helps them to embed it, remember it and be more conscious of it. Throughout the afternoon, I will write their observations and comments on the flip chart.

I begin with a direct question.

"What impact do you want to have on your customers?"

Although the question is straightforward, it takes a few moments of thought before they start to respond:

"I want to increase my sales."

"I want to get more yeses."

"I want more referrals."

"I want to be trusted."

"I want them to buy more."

These are the same identifiers that Adrienne described in her first call, when she told me the sales team were not realising their full potential. I'm pleased to hear that the team have now identified these themselves.

I turn to Ros. "Think about an opportunity to make an impact on your customer. When will that be?"

"Obviously, on my calls."

"Right. What is it you're wanting to achieve?"

"Well, I really want to delight them. I want them to give good feedback about me. Ultimately, I want them to buy from me."

Turning to the group, I say, "Everything we say and do has an impact on our customer and their decision to buy. Our interactions, on the phone and face to face in customer sales meetings and so on, all change what happens next."

"In that case," Ros says, "I want more of it. I want to make more of an impact."

"Brilliant. To have more impact, we need to start by looking at your personal authority."

Developing personal authority

I refer to the flip chart again. "When I say **personal authority**, what do I mean by that?"

Ros asks, "Is it my confidence?"

"This whole exercise is about your confidence. When I say authority, what do you think?"

Naomi says, "My job, my title."

"Partly. Your job title or role is not your personal authority; it's your given authority. You can use it alongside your personal authority."

Peter thinks for a moment and then asks, "Is it the things you know?"

"Exactly. It's your knowledge. What else could it be? If you want more impact, what would you need to draw on?"

"My skills?" asks Carl.

"Yes. It's everything you bring with you from the past. It's your experience, your record, your reputation, your network, your credentials – all those things. Nobody can take them away from you. Tell me, what are you known for?"

In asking this I am stimulating the group to start thinking about their past achievements.

Steve jumps in. "So, we send everybody to Naomi who wants to buy a Mac. She's the Apple queen of the business, I'd say."

I ask them to consider this further. "What does Naomi have, then, that you don't have?"

"She's got knowledge."

"But what else has she got?"

Carl says, "She's got a reputation."

Naomi is visibly surprised. "Oh my God, is that what you all think?"

"Of course – we always send our Mac customers to you."

The group are suddenly engaged with the concept that they all have some kind of personal authority. They share their respective qualifications, their latest research and their achievements. These are things they never really knew about each other. The energy levels in the room begin to rise and there is a genuine sense of excitement in this learning about their colleagues. They are beginning to see how their personal authority can connect with their jobs, but they are also understanding each other more than ever before. It's a happy effect of getting to understand themselves.

Once they have all had their chance to share this information, I ask, "Where does personal authority sit? Past, present or future?"

They all unanimously agree "In the past," and I add that

to the personal power triangle under "personal authority". The list of qualities they've identified now includes:

- Knowledge
- Skills
- Experience
- Record
- Network

"Is personal authority really about self-confidence?" asks Carl.

I answer, "Yes. Self-confidence can come from remembering and thinking about your personal authority. Perceived confidence comes when you mention your personal authority. If you say 'In my experience...' that indicates that you have experience. Or 'An article I read recently...' shows that you have some knowledge."

Developing charisma

I ask the group to focus on the personal power triangle again. I explain that if they want to have more impact, they must start by drawing on their personal authority. They can then develop their charisma. – speaking simply and clearly with conviction, listening and asking powerful questions, and knowing when not to speak. By using the right words, inflection, tone of voice and body language, they will have more personal presence, charisma and conviction.

I explain that charisma is something you can learn. It's an aspect of your personality that can be developed through how you communicate and how you use your interpersonal skills.

The mood is light in the room, but the point I am making is serious.

"What is charisma?" I ask.

"Our words?" replies Peter.

"Yes," I smile, but I'm looking for more. "What do our words need to be if we are going to be charismatic?"

The group fire responses back at me.

"Yes, you're all right. Our words need to be strong, relevant, crystal clear, succinct and accurate. What about how we speak?" I probe deeper.

Zoë answers with a question. "Do you mean our tone?"

"Yes. We need to make sure our voice sounds interested and enthusiastic."

"Is it the emphasis we put on certain words?" asks Carl.

"Right again. It's also our speed, volume and even when we pause." I reply.

Everyone in the group is nodding.

"So if what we say is the words, then how we say it is the music," I confirm.

"So is dance our body language?" Ros asks, wide-eyed with interest.

"It is," I say, "and this is particularly important if you're meeting face to face or making a presentation. Our posture, eye contact, facial expressions, movement and gestures are all part of our dance."

"But Carl and I don't meet people face to face. We're on the phone with customers, so how does that work for us?" Ros enquires.

"Just because you're selling on the phone doesn't mean that your body language won't affect the way you sound," Naomi jumps in.

"You're right, Naomi," I confirm. "Customers pick up these tones really quickly. When a customer is talking to you over the phone, can you tell when they're smiling?" I ask.

"Definitely." Carl nods.

"Your body language, gestures, posture and facial expressions all affect how you are coming across."

Ros nods in agreement too.

I continue, "In sales we need to speak with conviction. If we don't sound sure, our customers won't be convinced. Have you ever heard someone speaking whose sentences rise at the end?"

"Yes," Peter says. "My niece does it all the time. She's a really bright teenager, but she never sounds like she means anything she says. All her sentences go up at the end. Everything sounds like a question, even when it's a statement."

"Exactly," I agree. "To be convincing our sentences must go down at the end. Not much, but just enough for people to know we are sure about what we are saying."

I invite the group to try this out and by the end of the

brief exercise they all realise the subtle nuances of being convincing.

Making the impact you want

"So in summary," I continue, "this means that our words, music and dance all have to match. If you aren't crystal clear, you don't sound passionate or sincere and you don't express enthusiasm with your face and body, you'll diminish your charisma and conviction. Ultimately, your personal power will weaken significantly."

"Oh my God!" Ros interjects again, "I can totally see that if my tone of voice isn't right, my impact drops. If my body language isn't right, my impact drops."

"I'm still not sure how this all links in with my personal authority though, Jamie. Can you explain that?" asks Naomi.

"Yes. You can have all the personal authority in the world, all the knowledge and experience, but unless you can show this in what you say, how you say it and how you are when you say it, your impact is not going to be as strong as you think. It's like saying to a customer, 'In my experience, when other customers buy a GoPro, they also buy a spare battery pack so they don't have to worry when they go on long trips.'"

The group nod at how convincing I sound.

"Notice how I didn't just speak with charisma and conviction – I also added my personal authority. When you do this, you're much more likely to be influential," I emphasise.

"Remember not to go into too much detail – we don't need all your knowledge. Pause regularly and listen to what your customer is saying. Watch your posture and facial expressions. Don't forget that your words, music and dance have to match if you are to be believed."

Pointing to the flip chart again, I wrap the discussion up. "Your personal power is three things. Remembering and expressing your personal authority. Making sure that your words, music and dance match and that you speak with conviction. And that you use these things to change what happens next – to make the impact you want."

The group take a five-minute energiser break.

Communication styles

When they return, I get the group to complete an exercise in their participant workbooks. Individually they choose a selection of words which describe how they communicate when selling. The results show them their communication style:

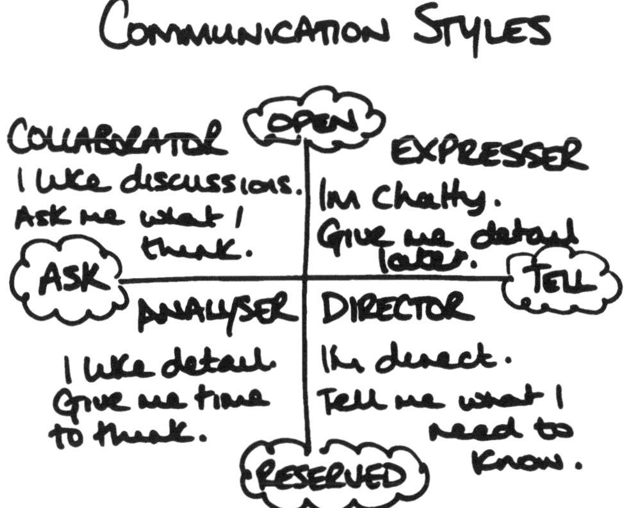

I explain.

"**Analysers** tend to be prepared. They can be reserved, they prefer accurate, realistic information and they tend not to wing it. Also, they love detail and they need time to think, read, clarify and so on.

"**Expressers** are often warm and friendly and show people that they care. They don't usually like the detail – so if detail is important, they appreciate you sending it by email. They like to be asked questions and they like to be able to finish what they're saying.

"**Collaborators** are people-oriented. They ask questions and are more interested in having a dialogue and including others. They like to be asked for their opinions, they prefer inclusivity, they're not particularly demanding and they appreciate being given time to think or discuss the matter at hand.

"**Directors**, as the description suggests, have quite a direct manner. On the surface, they can seem quite abrupt or uninterested. They're not particularly keen on chit-chat and they usually want to get straight down to business. They're more interested in results and less interested in the detail that led to those results."

Peter rolls his eyes. "Oh, I know where this is going to go. I know what I'm going to come out as. Analyser – it's obvious."

A few moments later everyone's results are in. I turn to Peter. "What did you come out as?"

"Like I said, analyser. No surprises there."

"Let's look at what that means. Analysers are – as you'd expect – analytical. They're usually quite accurate and they're problem solvers. They love to gather information and enjoy covering all the detail. They take their time with things. They have clear expectations and they're very proud of their work. But generally, they don't talk about personal things."

"Oh my God, that is so totally you, Pete," Ros squeals.

Peter is visibly surprised by my summing up of him. "That's amazing."

The others are suddenly excited and intrigued to find out what each other's results show. Steve turns to Ros. "What have you come up as? I bet you're an expresser." And "I bet Carl's a director."

"It's obvious Carl's a director," says Naomi. "That's why he gets on so well with Andrew."

"Actually, I'm a collaborator," says Ros. "What does that mean?"

"You don't go it alone. You're consistent and reliable. You like to work with others but you don't offer your opinion often. You're diligent and dependable, and you prefer harmony to conflict. In general, you come across as adaptable, calm, thoughtful, sympathetic and non-confrontational. Do we all agree that sums up Ros?"

There is total agreement in the room, as Ros blushes slightly.

"I want us to look at what this all means," I say, "and how you communicate with each other, for starters."

I turn to Carl. "If you're going to communicate with Ros, knowing what you know now, what's this told you?"

He thinks for a moment, and then says, "Well, normally, I'd be very direct. But Ros, reading this, likes somebody to be non-threatening. She likes people to ask her opinion. She likes to be inclusive and not demanding. She likes to have time to think. Whereas before, I would've been all guns blazing and not really thought about how she'd like me to talk to her."

"What are you learning from this?"

Carl is quick to answer. "I've realised that I have to flex my style to influence another style."

"Precisely. Now imagine, everyone, what that can do when you're speaking with a customer. Zoë, you spoke about clients being demanding on the phone. Your results here show you're an expresser. That means when you encounter a customer who prefers a director style of communication, if you just flex your own style to be more direct, you'll find that you're more connected to the customer so you're more likely to influence them. The customer will feel that they're talking to someone on their wavelength."

"For once," Carl chips in, much to everyone's amusement.

I summarise. "Knowing your own communication style is interesting, but being able to flex your style to match your customers' communication needs is essential if you want to become much more influential."

To give them all a chance to practise flexing their communication style, I give them a set of realistic role-play scenarios. In pairs, one person plays the role of a customer displaying one of the four communication styles and the other plays the salesperson.

One at a time, the salespeople have to first identify the customer's communication style and then flex their own style to build rapport.

Afterwards, the group reflect.

"Hmm. It sounds easier in theory than it is in practice," Steve speaks up.

"Yes. You really have to tune into the customer and listen to how they're speaking," Ros agrees. "That's hard if it's us doing most of the talking."

Carl follows. "Strangely, when I flexed my communication style to match Zoë's when she was playing the customer, I felt like I was having more of an impact."

"You were," Zoë confirms. "I was playing an analyser and the level of detail you went into was just right, I think."

"I'm glad this exercise has worked for you. Don't expect to be brilliant at it overnight, though. It takes practice," I reassure.

The group take some time to write the fear-free feedback they were given into their booklets.

I look at the clock and then down at my trainer plan. It's time to wrap up day one.

The trust equation

Homework is always greeted with a collective groan – it suggests to the trainees that they can't just walk out of the room and leave the learning behind. But as I hand out the paperwork, I assure the group that this is a quick, simple exercise. I explain that all they need to do is spend five minutes at home considering the four questions in the trust equation exercise. I stress that they must answer with total honesty, otherwise the exercise won't tell them where their opportunity to improve is.

They'll score themselves out of ten for each part of the trust equation:

THE TRUST EQUATION

YOUR TRUSTWORTHINESS RATING:

LOW TRUST FACTOR

HIGH TRUST FACTOR

−30 −20 −10 Ø +10 +20 +30

1. **How credible are you?** This measures how much your customers can trust your ability to do what you say you can. Rate yourself out of 10. Answer honestly.

2. **How reliable are you?** This is about consistency. It measures how much your customers can trust you to do what you say. Rate yourself out of 10. Answer honestly.

3. **How intimate are you?** This is about your closeness to your customers. It measures warmth and how much they can trust you when they share personal information. Rate yourself out of 10. Answer honestly.

4. **How self-oriented are you?** This is partly about whether you focus on commission or the customer, but it's also about how much your customers feel that you place your own interests above theirs. This can even be a feeling that you are selling to them. Rate yourself out of 10 and multiply by 3. Remember, be honest!

"To calculate your trustworthiness score, you add your credibility rating, your reliability rating and your intimacy rating together, giving you a sub-total score out of thirty. Then you calculate your self-orientation rating and multiply it by three. You then subtract this number from your sub-total score, giving you a total trustworthiness rating. This means that your total trustworthiness rating could be as high as thirty if you scored ten on credibility, reliability and intimacy and zero on self-orientation. Or it could be as low as minus thirty, if you scored zero on credibility, reliability or intimacy and thirty on self-orientation."

"It's not very scientific, is it?" Steve comments.

"No, Steve," I agree with him and smile broadly, "it's definitely not an exact science. But it's a good way of examining your own trustworthiness, which is something we very rarely do."

I explain that the next day we will examine their individual results to reveal their overall trustworthiness score. It's a simple – yet profoundly revealing – exercise. Because it's not time-consuming or demanding, the trainees are all happy to give it their best shot.

Overall, their day has been more about fun than hardship, helped by my relaxed but focused delivery. They don't quite know where this is all heading yet, but they feel they've learned something and they're beginning to find out how to put it into practice.

What they don't know yet is what I have planned for tomorrow – and they will be blown away by what they discover next.

CHAPTER 4

THE WORKSHOP – DAY TWO

The trust equation – homework results

The next morning, I'm pleased that the whole group has returned with their completed homework. I open the session with:

"Tell me, who can I trust?"

Everyone raises their hand, although I notice that Steve does so a little less enthusiastically. "Let's start by sharing what we found and whether anything surprised you when you were answering the questions."

"The questions really made me think about myself," said Peter.

"I was thinking about it all last night," adds Naomi.

"I didn't like answering the self-orientation question, because it made me question my motives. I don't often do that." Everybody laughs, because they all know that about Carl.

Steve comments, "I thought it was kind of an interesting exercise, but I'm not sure I see the point of it."

"That's okay, Steve. As long as you all tried to answer the questions honestly, this is going to tell you where your opportunity to improve is."

I explain that the original trust equation is a formula created by Charles H. Green, and I have adapted it slightly. I now help the group analyse their results, which gives me a valuable snapshot of how trusted they are as individuals.

I ask Ros about her score. I already know that she is a positive person with a natural, bubbly personality that is immediately engaging. The group listen to her with interest – and some relief that they weren't asked first.

Overall, Ros has scored very well, so she's surprised when Zoë offers her an observation. "Oh, you scored yourself quite high on reliability. I wasn't expecting that. There've been a couple of times when you've not completed an order."

Ros is certain she had answered her questions honestly, but another person perceives her reliability differently. This takes the discussion exactly where I want it to head, since it opens the group up to thinking objectively about how trusted they are.

Carl has scored himself low on intimacy. "You know what, saying this now is quite hard for me. I don't reveal much about myself."

I am quick to reassure him. "That's great honesty, Carl, and I think it's a good observation. To share it is fantastic. Obviously, you need to start working out how to increase your intimacy score."

"You say that, Carl," Naomi steps in, "but what's interesting is, you've actually just shared quite an intimate observation about yourself – it's ironic that you're not very intimate."

The group agrees.

I continue, "When you show yourselves as vulnerable, your customers trust you more and are more likely to show their vulnerability too. As long as it's appropriate, that makes it a lot easier to build a relationship with a customer."

"But what about your self-orientation scores?" I ask.

For a moment, the group hesitates. Then Steve speaks up.

"I rated myself fairly low to start with," he begins, "because I felt I was very customer-focused. But the more I thought about it, the more I realised that I do tend to focus on just getting through the day. By late afternoon I definitely become more of an order- taker because I process each customer quickly so that I can leave on time."

"And how does that impact your overall trustworthiness, Steve?" I enquire.

"Well, after I multiplied my self-orientation rating by three, I could see how I'm having a negative impact on how much customers feel they can trust me," he admits.

"Why do we have to multiply the self-orientation score by three?" Naomi asks.

Before I can respond, Carl answers.

"Because being self-focused damages how much we're trusted." He looks at me for assurance and I nod.

Others in the group offer up their self-orientation scores and share their insights as to why they've given themselves the rating they have. I listen carefully as they each discuss what they do that makes them self-focused rather than customer-focused.

It's always fascinating for me to see the light bulbs come on in the eyes of my participants.

Overnight, much of what we talked about yesterday has begun to take hold in their minds. Where I previously detected some resistance, there is now a growing understanding. Where there was confidence, there is a realisation that this alone may not be enough. As a result, none of the trainees are starting day two as top dog or bottom of the class. The intelligent simplicity and personal depth of my sales training process mean everyone begins this second day on a level playing field. They've been prompted not only to reflect on their own behaviour patterns and techniques but also to see themselves through the eyes of their colleagues and customers.

I wrap up this section of the workshop.

"How we see our own trustworthiness is often different from how our customers perceive it. We need to make sure that our customers feel that we are completely credible, that we know what we are taking about, that we are reliable and that we do what we say we will. To be seen as intimate, we need to be comfortable about sharing information about ourselves.

"But don't forget that while all these things are great, they can be damaged by our self-orientation. If the customer gets a hint that we don't have their best interests at heart, our credability, reliability and intimacy will be damaged."

FAB – features, advantages and benefits

Every salesperson can sell the features of a product. Fewer sell the advantages that each feature brings. Even fewer sell the benefits to the customer. By the end of this module, I want the sales team to understand that each product has an advantage and a benefit that they can link direct to the customer.

I step over to the flip chart and start writing.

F for **feature** – what is the feature?

A for **advantage** – what does the feature do?

B for **benefit** – how does that benefit me, the customer?

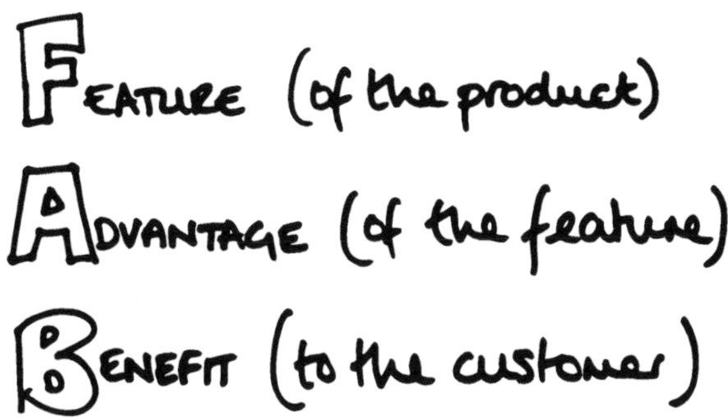

I begin by asking them to shout out any of the products they sell.

Continuing the theme from yesterday, they settle on the GoPro.

I instruct, “Describe why a typical customer may want to buy a GoPro.”

“Because they’re going on an adventure holiday and they want to attach one to their bike or helmet,” Peter starts us off.

“So what happens next?”

“We sell them a GoPro because that’s what they want,” Zoë continues.

"Exactly. You sell them a GoPro because it's small, portable and durable and that's what the customer wants. Those are the features the customer is looking for. But what would happen if you explained in more detail about the GoPro range? If you told the customer about the advantages the GoPro range offers?"

"You mean, like waterproofing?" Peter asks.

"Great. The GoPro has a waterproof seal. Is that a feature, advantage or benefit?"

"A feature?" Zoë is hesitant.

"Yes. What's the advantage?" I probe.

"The advantage is it can be used in the sea," Ros jumps in.

"Good. So if it can be used underwater, what's the benefit to the customer?" I explore deeper.

Naomi takes a stab at it. "Is the benefit that the customer can take photos and videos of some of the most memorable and amazing aspects of their holiday?"

"Right. Everything they do in or under the water can be filmed – something they've never been able to do before.

Keep going. Focus on benefits." I encourage them to go further.

"They'd be able to use it more often and they'd only need one GoPro, because they can use it in and out of water. That means it's going to save them money, they don't need to buy two – that's the benefit." Carl smiles, knowing he has grasped this concept quickly.

"Another benefit may be kudos," Steve adds.

Naomi offers another example as the penny begins to drop for her. "If I've found out from the customer that it's a once-in-a-lifetime trip or special anniversary holiday, I'd then suggest they go for the high-definition version, so they can remember it in crystal-clear vision."

"You've hit the nail on the head, Naomi. In a nutshell, benefits are what a customer values.

"These are boiled down to three things… PPI."

PPI – productivity, profitability and image

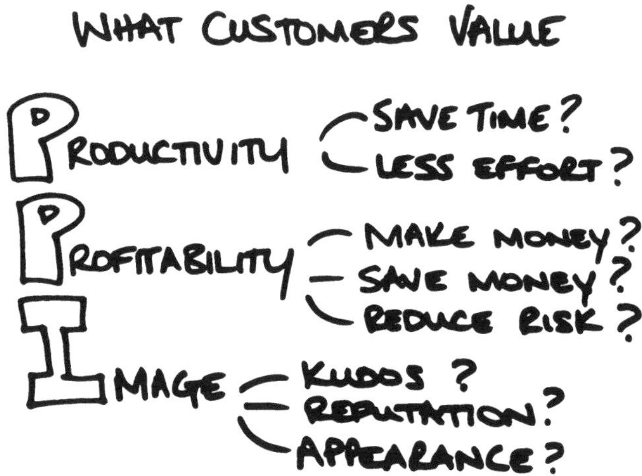

I explain.

"**Productivity**: Customers want to be more productive – to save time and effort.

"**Profitability**: Customers want to make money, save money or reduce risk.

"**Image**: Customers value their kudos, their reputation or their appearance.

"Once you've engaged with your customer, discovered what their holiday is all about and discussed all the advantages of the various features, you can recommend the model that meets needs that they might never have considered, emphasising what benefits it will bring."

For the first time today, Naomi looks pleased with herself as this new understanding hits home. I can see her colleagues are also beginning to piece together the bigger sales picture as they talk about the opportunities they've missed or the ones they'll grab in the future.

Carl asks me, "So how do you link the features and advantages to the benefits?"

"Well, a big part of that is knowing your products inside out. But what's just as important is being able to listen to what your customer is saying so you can link the features of the product with the benefits to the customer. Let's go there now."

Active listening and powerful questions

"What is the definition of **active listening**?"

"Not falling asleep?" Zoë quips, and everyone laughs.

I laugh with them. "That does often help – thanks, Zoë.

But let's try to get to the meaning of this. What is active listening?"

The group brainstorm a few responses:

"Paying attention?"

"Looking someone in the eye?"

"Not interrupting?"

"It's all of those," I agree, "but it's more about showing that you are intelligently listening to what is and isn't being said.

"When you're dealing with a customer, are you really listening or are you just waiting to speak?"

"If it's Ros, they won't get a word in edgeways," Zoë winks.

"Ha, ha! So speaks the expresser," Ros rolls her eyes.

I continue "Have you ever been telling someone about the holiday you've been on – and they come back with, 'Oh, I've been there. I went for a month. I did this and I did that...'?"

"That sounds like Angie in accounts."

"I haven't met Angie," I say, "but generally speaking, I tend to avoid this kind of person. They're often considered to be conversation hijackers."

"Yep, that's Angie," Steve chuckles.

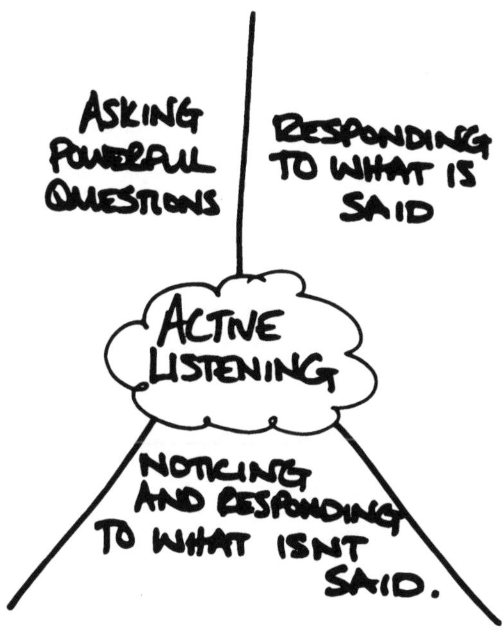

"Even when we think we're listening, we're usually trying to think of the next thing we're going to say, and when we do that we don't really hear what the other person is saying. When you're speaking with your customer, you have to focus completely on what's being said. You can't be entering data in your computer. You can't be thinking about what's coming up next. You have to ask great questions based on what they've said and then listen to the answers that are coming back to you."

"And then ask more questions?" adds Peter.

"You could. But probably not the questions that you planned to ask. What I'm saying here is that to show that you're actively listening you need to ask a question based on what you've just heard."

"You mean exploring what the customer just said rather than simply moving on to the next question?" asks Naomi.

"Right. But why is that difficult?" I ask.

"Because we second-guess what they're about to say. We think we already know what they mean." Steve looks thoughtful as he contemplates this for a moment.

"Exactly," I nod. "Asking questions based on what you've just heard is powerful because you end up knowing much more about what a customer wants and needs. With the extra knowledge you've gleaned from probing, you can sell them the benefits of the product, not the features or advantages."

"I like this," says Steve. "It means I can link my vast product knowledge to what a customer is telling me."

"Yes. And what a customer tells you comes from what you ask them and whether you truly listen to what they are saying," I emphasise.

"And I thought active listening was just repeating what you'd heard," Naomi interjects.

"Well, that's part of showing that you're listening too," I continue. "Repeating back part of the conversation, or even summing up what you just heard, is still active listening. Your customer will get a sense that you were listening carefully to everything they just said if you briefly play it back to them, especially if they've been speaking for a minute or two."

"Earlier on, you said that active listening is also responding to what *isn't* said. What did you mean by that?" Zoë asks.

"Well," I bounce Zoë's question back to the group, "do you think it's possible to listen to what isn't being said?"

"Yes – by reading someone's body language," Carl replies.

"Good. How else?" I ask.

"Do you mean reading between the lines of what they *are* saying?" Naomi offers.

"You've both got it." I smile at them. "Noticing and responding to body language, facial expressions and verbal cues, like hesitation or silence, is part of active listening. And so is noticing and responding to what is implied or hinted at. In other words, reading between the lines."

"Can you give us an example, please?" requests Steve.

"Of course," I nod. "Let's say you're chatting to a customer during a sales meeting and they look at their watch while you're speaking. You notice them do it, but do you respond or just carry on talking?"

"Well, I'd definitely notice it, but I'm not sure what I'd say," Steve replies honestly.

"How about, 'Is now a good time?'" Ros suggests.

"I like that," I smile. "So we've noticed the customer look at their watch, we've asked them if now is a good time and they say, 'Actually, I have to make an urgent call. Sorry.' What do you do?"

"Give them a few minutes to make the urgent call," Carl confirms.

"Right. But so what? Why is this useful to you?"

"Because if we notice but don't respond, the customer won't be listening to all the great things we'd be telling them. Half their mind would be on the call they have to make. We'd be wasting our breath." Peter is pleased he has grasped the idea so quickly.

"Spot on, Peter," I say, equally pleased with how quickly the group are picking up these concepts. "Here are some things you can say to show you've noticed what isn't being said." I show them the following list:

- It sounds like another phone is ringing there. Do you need to answer it?
- I can hear that you're in the middle of something else. Is now a good time?
- You sound unsure. What questions do you have?
- Go on, what were you about to say?
- One thing you haven't mentioned is...
- You sound annoyed about that. Tell me more about what's gone wrong.
- Am I right in saying that you're also having a problem with...?

I hand out an exercise on active listening and the group dive into it with enthusiasm. I listen carefully and monitor what they say and do during each scenario. I encourage them to give each other fear-free feedback on how they are using their active listening skills.

By the end of the session the group are buzzing. I summarise in the usual way.

"Active listening is showing your customer that you're listening to them properly. The aim of active listening is two-fold:

1. You want your customer to know that you are genuinely interested in what they are saying.
2. You want to be able to extract as much information from them as possible.

"You do this in three ways:

1. By asking powerful questions
2. Through the responses that you give to what is said
3. By noticing and responding to what isn't said."

Peter says, "I can see how this can work for me. I would have missed all this previously."

"The good news is, Peter, that we can do much more with the extra information we get through listening. Let me explain – who here has heard of cross-selling and up-selling?"

Cross-selling and up-selling

Ros instantly throws her hand up. "We do cross-selling already. We always try to push a customer to buy something extra, like memory cards or batteries."

"Or we up-sell and get them to buy a more expensive model or version of what they were originally looking for," Peter adds.

"It's how we bump up our commission," says Naomi.

"Well, there's a couple of problems with what you've just told me. Firstly, trust. If the customer gets a sense that you're not being customer-oriented, they'll see your up-selling or cross-selling as a ploy that benefits you, not them. Don't forget that even a hint of self-orientation is incredibly damaging to your overall trust. And secondly, if you *push* a customer to buy more or better, you're likely to meet with resistance.

"It would be better to use your active listening skills to listen out for hooks. Later in the conversation, you can come back to the hooks you've heard and use them as a legitimate way of offering the customer something more or better than what they came looking for."

"Here's an example of what I mean," I continue. "Imagine a customer is buying a drone for a wedding they're going to. They want to get some unique aerial shots of the venue, the gardens and the bride and groom. They start by enquiring about one of the basic models you stock. Listening carefully, you ask questions to uncover more information. Slowly you find out that it's the wedding of their closest friend and it's taking place at a castle in Scotland this summer. As a present to the bride and groom, the customer is going to edit the footage and publish it on a website for all the guests to view. They've never used a drone before and they don't have video-editing experience. How would you up-sell or cross-sell?"

"Well if that was me, I'd want something that's easy to fly," Ros is first to speak.

"They need the higher-spec drone with the auto-fly setting," says Carl.

"And if they want to impress the bride and groom and the guests, they should go for the high-definition video model," Zoë adds.

"Okay," I say, "now you're thinking about the customer, not your bonus. You've used your active listening skills to up-sell. How could you cross-sell as well?"

"I know," says Naomi. "We can encourage them to buy an extra battery pack, because if it's a summer wedding it's likely to be outdoors so there might not be many charging points."

"Good idea, Naomi, but I can go one better than that," Steve grins. "How about user-friendly video-editing software to make the final video really easy to produce and upload?"

"You've all nailed it." I am delighted.

"I'd always seen up-selling and cross-selling as hidden ways of getting customers to part with more money," Peter contemplates. "I hadn't thought that they would see me as sneaky and untrustworthy."

"Peter, this is all about recognising our intention, because whether we like it or not, our intention is often more apparent to our customers than we think it is. Up-selling and cross-selling are about genuinely taking an interest, listening carefully, and becoming less self-oriented," I confirm. "Instead of being driven by your commission or targets, be driven by asking questions that help the customer tell you about their needs, wants and wishes. Then, given your product knowledge, you can suggest extras and encourage upgrades."

The group are enthused and I let them chat about their new way of thinking while I pour myself some water.

"But this doesn't stop customers from asking us difficult questions," says Naomi.

I sip my water and smile. "You've read my mind, Naomi, because that's exactly what we are going to be discussing next."

Handling objections

"Firstly, let me ask you all a question," I start. "What are the most common objections you face?"

"They often say that they need time to think before buying," says Peter.

"'This is outside my budget,'" adds Zoë.

"'I don't need one with such high spec,'" adds Carl.

"Okay," I explain, "if you're getting these objections at the end, you need to stop and ask yourself, 'How have we got this far in the conversation and I haven't picked up on this already – through answers to my questions, what isn't being said or the signals they're giving me?'"

"So are you saying that we want to avoid getting objections at the end?" asks Naomi.

"That's exactly what I'm saying." I am serious. "If you've got to this part of the sales conversation and suddenly your customer is saying they can't afford what you've suggested, you haven't done a good enough job of:

- listening to them
- explaining the benefit of the product in terms they value, and
- signposting the increase in price as you go."

"Jamie, can you give us an example?" Carl pipes up.

"Okay. Let's take our previous example of buying a drone to shoot a wedding video. At a basic level you'll be asking things like, 'Is this a present for the bride and groom?' Yes.

'Is this something that you want to impress them with?' Yes. 'Let me show you a sample video – is that what you'd like to do?' Yes. 'Well, to do that, you'll need the high-definition fish-eye lens. Which means you'll need to consider that in your budget.'"

I continue. "Your customer is much more likely to register this during the conversation and be willing to rethink their budget, and it's less likely to pop up as an objection at the end."

"This is really useful. I've never thought of addressing objections throughout the conversation to prevent them coming up at the end," Zoë opens up.

"I can't promise they'll never come up at the end," I add, "but if you put yourself in the customer's shoes and really listen to what they're telling you, even non-verbally, you'll be tuning into your customer in ways you've never done before. This stronger connection will make you feel more confident about uncovering objections and handling them as you go, rather than ignoring them and hoping they won't ever surface."

"But I always seem to get the pushy customers who are never happy with what I'm offering and ask for the earth," Ros complains. "What am I meant to do with them?"

I turn to the next page of the flip chart, which reads **the saying no formula**.

"Ros, your timing is perfect. Let's have a tea break and then I'll take you through the model."

The saying no formula

As the group settle down with their cups of tea and coffee, I reveal the full formula that I hinted at before the break.

THE SAYING NO FORMULA

EMPATHY
+
"Its not possible..."
+
REAL REASON
+
OPTION
+
"Its not possible..."

"Let's give this some context," I begin. "A customer is asking for something that we simply can't give them – a discount or expensive extras thrown in for free."

"It happens to me all the time," admits Ros.

"Firstly, let's explore empathy. In this context, what empathy can we show our customers when they ask for more?"

Naomi responds. "Could we say something like, 'I see where you're coming from – it's nice to get a discount on such a large purchase, isn't it?'"

"Great," I smile. "This is just a brief sentence to let them know you understand their position. Then the words are, 'It's not possible...' followed by the real reason why."

"Why not just say that I can't?" challenges Steve.

"Because when people hear 'I can't' they think we're saying 'I won't,'" responds Carl.

"True," I agree. "And 'It's not possible...' depersonalises your refusal. It's like saying the circumstances won't allow it. Make sure you give the real, honest reason why not. Customers will know when you're just being difficult or telling fibs."

"What options can we give?" asks Zoë.

"Tell them the alternative thing that you can do. Or the small version of their bigger ask."

"You mean like giving them an extension to their warranty?" asks Naomi. "That doesn't cost us much at all."

"Actually, customers really like it when I do that," Peter agrees.

"Great suggestion," I confirm. "The options are ideal if they are low cost to you and FusionTech and high value to your customer.

"Finally, you repeat the refusal by saying, 'But it's not possible to give you the extra discount.' You emphasise that what they're asking for is not going to happen."

Ros looks up from her booklet as she captures the key learning points. "I think you just changed my life, Jamie!"

"Well, it *is* a powerful way of saying no. And in my experience, when you stick to the formula you protect the customer relationship. As with all these things, it's important to practise and get some feedback, so let's give this a go."

I kick off an activity where each team member decides on a realistic customer request. They take it in turns to practise using the saying no formula. They get some valuable feedback from one another on how they use each element of the formula and on their words, music and dance.

Closing the sale

I smile to myself. It's getting late in the afternoon now and this group aren't flagging one bit. The team are on fire and still seem to have energy for more.

"So, how would you close the sale?" I throw this open question to the group. I can tell in an instant that this is a topic they feel less confident about.

"I'd ask them if they want to add a warranty so that they're covered," says Peter, after several seconds of hesitation.

"Tell me more," I explore.

"Well, it's something I learned once as a sneaky way of getting a customer to agree to the sale." Peter cringes inwardly as he hears his own words.

"And does that method always work?" I smile.

"Sometimes," Peter is honest, "but I do feel that more often than not, it raises more objections than it avoids."

"I've used that one a few times too," admits Zoë, "but now I think about it, I'm basically saying that I don't trust you to go ahead with buying these products, so I'm going to trick you into it. I'm damaging trust, aren't I?"

I nod and simply say, "Yes, you are."

I give them a moment to reflect. Then I ask, "How do you think this makes your customers feel?"

"That we're self-oriented. That we only care about the sale," Carl says.

"Yeah. That we aren't really interested in them or their needs – we just want them to buy," Naomi adds.

"Think back to the trust equation," I point to the flip chart on the wall. "All that credibility you've been building, your reliability and intimacy – all slip away in the final moments, because you've exposed your true motive."

"But we're a sales team," Steve challenges. "That's what

we're ultimately building up to – the closing phase. How else are we meant to get them to part with their money?"

I nod. "I can understand why you think that, Steve. I thought that way for many years too. But why have I called this entire concept socially intelligent selling?"

The room falls silent as they mull my question over in the context of the current discussion.

I wait for someone to speak. It's important that they reach this conclusion themselves. I don't want to lead them too much.

Ros eventually speaks up. "Do you mean that if we've related to the customer and done enough discovery, we won't need clumsy gimmicks to entice them into buying?"

"Go on," I dig deeper.

This time, Zoë responds. "That we've asked questions to find common ground and build a stronger, thicker relationship rope. So they trust us much earlier in the conversation."

"Yes. I'm liking this. Keep going," I encourage.

"That we've asked the right discovery questions and really listened to the answers," Naomi joins in, "so they feel we've taken a genuine interest in them and taken time to carefully understand what they need."

"Good. Give me more." I smile.

"That we've linked the advantages of the product to the benefits this specific customer is looking for most," Carl states.

"And that we've handled their objections with patience and empathy throughout the conversation," Peter speaks up.

"You are all right. And thank you – you've actually just recapped this whole course." I laugh.

"Are you saying that if our customers like us and trust us, we won't need to close?" Steve asks, with a hint of cynicism in his voice.

Before I can answer him, Ros exclaims, "Oh my goodness, Steve, you're right! This is like selling, but without the selling."

I smile at Ros and then turn to Steve. "What I'm saying, Steve, is that if you get to what you're calling the closing phase – which I believe we should think of as the end of the relationship-building conversation – and your customer backs off, there was probably a sign much earlier on that you didn't spot, or did spot but ignored and pushed through."

The team nod as this message sinks in.

A lightbulb flickers on in Steve's eyes. "So if we're socially intelligent throughout the sales conversation – in the way that you've taught us – then the close comes from our customer, not from us."

"You've just hit the nail on the head," I congratulate him.

"So if we do this, will all our sales close themselves?" asks Naomi.

"I can't guarantee that," I reveal honestly, "but in my experience, if your customer doesn't close – for whatever reason – then because of the relationship you've just built with them, they'll either come back later or talk to their friends about you."

"So in a way, dead leads become our pipeline," Peter adds.

"Right," I nod. "It's win-win either way."

I am confident that the group have fully understood his concept. Now comes the *pièce de résistance*!

Putting it all together

I invite the group to look at the dozen or so flipcharts stuck to the walls of the training room.

"We've covered a lot in the last couple of days. And now it's your opportunity to practise what we've covered and get some useful feedback on how you come across."

"You mean more role play?" Steve doesn't sound thrilled.

"I do." I smile, knowing that there will be resistance in the room. "Here's what we're going to do."

I reveal one last flip chart with a list of all the techniques they've covered on the course.

"I'll be a customer and one at a time, you'll come up and have a sales conversation with me. Afterwards, the rest of us will give you some feedback and you can chose who goes next."

"I'll go first," Ros' hand shoots up. "I want to get this over and done with."

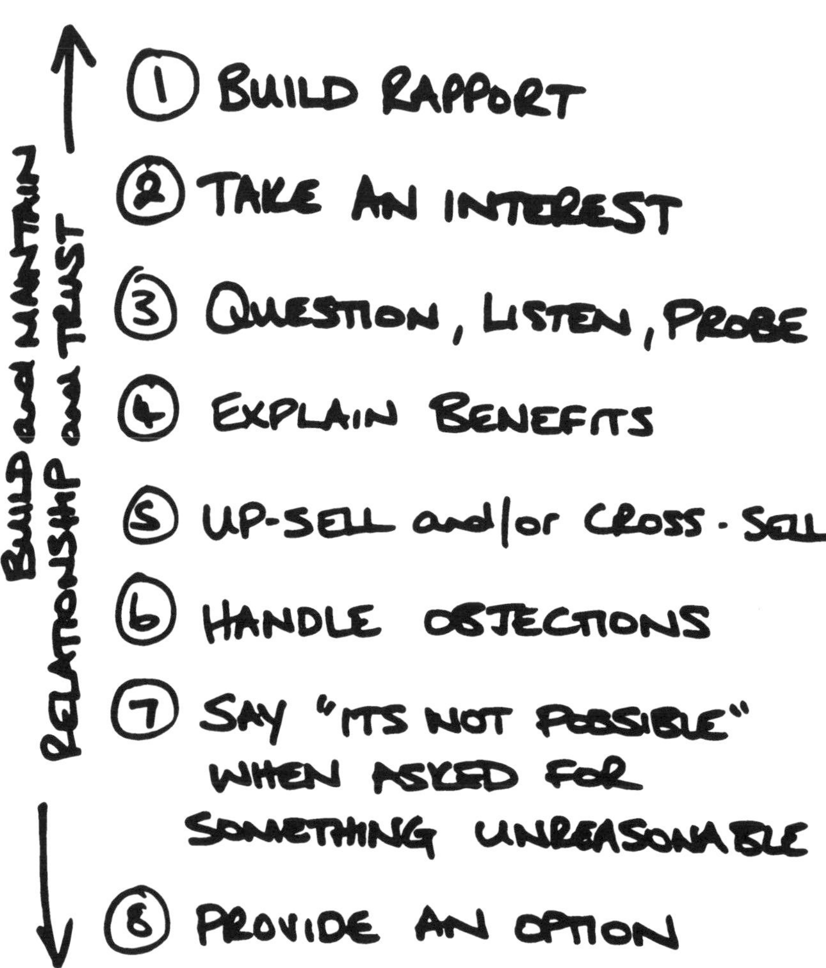
PUTTING IT ALL TOGETHER
BUILD and MAINTAIN RELATIONSHIP and TRUST
① BUILD RAPPORT
② TAKE AN INTEREST
③ QUESTION, LISTEN, PROBE
④ EXPLAIN BENEFITS
⑤ UP-SELL and/or CROSS-SELL
⑥ HANDLE OBJECTIONS
⑦ SAY "ITS NOT POSSIBLE" WHEN ASKED FOR SOMETHING UNREASONABLE
⑧ PROVIDE AN OPTION

"Liar," Carl laughs, "You'd do it all six times if you could. You love the limelight."

"That's true, actually," Ros laughs along with the others.

I give Ros a few moments to ground herself and mentally prepare for what is about to happen.

We launch into the role play. I am a customer buying a drone and Ros skilfully uses everything she has learned to conduct a socially intelligent sales conversation.

She takes time to build rapport and shows a genuine interest in what I am interested in. She questions, listens and probes. Once she has enough information she talks about the benefits of the product with real conviction. She asks more questions, listens and seizes an opportunity to up-sell. I respond with an objection and Ros listens, enquires, finds out what's behind the objection and addresses it. I push for a discount and Ros tells me that it's not possible, but offers me express delivery because she knows I need the drone this weekend.

She finishes the role play and turns to her teammates, who are all transfixed. She bows and they erupt into applause.

"That was great," declares Steve.

"How did you find that?" I ask.

"It was much easier than I thought it would be," Ros beams.

"Why do you think that was?" I enquire.

"It just seemed so natural and authentic," Ros answers.

"Exactly," I say. "Being socially intelligent is part of who we are as human beings. And it doesn't stop at selling. Being socially intelligent means that you're much more aware of how you come across in the conversations you have, fully tuning into the person you are speaking to and connecting to the purpose behind what's being discussed. Once you start using these skills in other aspects of life, it becomes a game changer."

The team are buzzing.

"Right, who's next?"

Steve jumps to his feet. "Me."

Outside the training room, Andrew stops by and presses his ear against the door. As he listens, he smiles to himself, barely recognising the confidence he hears in

Steve's voice. He returns to his office with a growing sense of satisfaction.

Several minutes later, the entire team have been through the exercise in putting it all together and each of them has received some valuable, fear-free feedback about what they are doing well and where they still have opportunities to improve.

Next, as the course concludes, I guide them through what I call **action planning**. This is an interactive exercise that helps them to decide their precise next steps. They come away with a plan of action that is strengthened by their teammates.

Finally, I ask them to revisit the gap analysis from yesterday morning.

1. How well do you relate to your customer?
2. How much do you discover about your customer's needs, wants and wishes?

Unanimously, they move their individual markers into the top right-hand area of the grid. The part that represents socially intelligent selling. I'm thrilled.

The models that I've presented, the self-reflection, the

exercises, the role-play activities and the fear-free feedback have culminated in a game-changing experience for them all.

*****

At the end of a long day, as the training room door flies open and the team head home, excited chatter fills the air.

Steve and Zoë hang back for a moment to speak with me. When I first met them, they were not particularly engaged with what I was saying. They were resistant to my efforts to introduce my teachings, in particular the softer skills involved with selling. Steve is first to speak:

"You know what, Jamie, this whole thing has been excellent. I'd be the first to admit I thought I knew it all before you showed up, but you've really opened my eyes."

Zoë agrees. "I could never understand why some of my clients just wouldn't sign on the dotted line – I was doing everything by the book and still some of them just wouldn't play ball. I've really gained a lot from this. I'm a confident person anyway, but maybe I need to be a little more understanding with some of my clients. Thank you."

I'm delighted. With Steve and Zoë in particular, I knew I faced some challenges. But their progress in the last couple of days, combined with the contributions of the whole team, has made the discussions invaluable to everyone.

"Sales at FusionTech were flatlining, despite all our efforts as a sales team. I have a feeling all that's about to change." Steve shakes my hand.

CHAPTER 5
THE FOLLOW-UP

One week later on a sunny Monday morning I meet with Adrienne and Andrew for a formal debrief and summary of the results and feedback from the training sessions.

Andrew is reading through the feedback forms from the participants, studying them carefully. After a few minutes, he looks at me quizzically over his glasses and says, with a little smile creeping across his face, "How have you done this? How much did you pay them to write this?"

Adrienne giggles uncharacteristically, which she turns into a cough. "You sound surprised, Andrew."

"Surprised? I hardly recognise these people."

It's obvious that Andrew has been caught a little off-guard by the results he's seeing from the feedback forms and graphs that I've presented him with. The results clearly show that the sales team he was once so concerned about have scored the workshop significantly above the industry average.

"I can't believe what I'm reading," he remarks, still looking at me over his glasses. "Look at this from Carl – and I quote – 'This has changed the way I think and the way I work. This is going to impact my career, not just my sales figures. I can't wait to put this into practice.'"

"I felt Carl really came a long way throughout the training," I said.

"Ros, she's saying 'This has changed my life.' Have you drugged these people, Jamie?"

Adrienne suppresses a laugh.

"As for Steve," Andrew continues reading the notes, "*Steve,* of all people; he's written here, 'I now have the tools to influence people in a way I never thought I could before.'"

"Steve was great in the training," I observe. "They all were. They challenged me at almost at every turn."

"Resistant?" enquired Adrienne.

"At first, yes," I reply. "But as the learning built and we started working through the exercises, you could see them accepting it more and more as the course progressed. By the end, their energy was electric."

"I'm glad to hear that," Andrew nods. "Talk me through what you did and how we've got to where we are today."

"To be honest, Andrew, they did all the work. All I did was share straightforward techniques for becoming a socially intelligent seller, then gave them honest, constructive feedback when they practised each skill."

"Ah yes, socially intelligent selling. They bought it?" Andrew leans forward.

"Of course. They realised the benefits of being authentically curious during sales conversations with their customers and building enough trust for the *customer* to close the sale, not them. It can take years to unravel clunky sales technique training and ingrained bad habits. I got them there in two days. My guess is, they won't just use this to sell – they'll be living it."

"So it's about being human rather than rehearsed?" Andrew raises an eyebrow.

"Right," I confirm. "Ironically, we had to rehearse being human – to bring back those natural inquisitive skills they were born with. They all encouraged each other with insightful feedback, which provided the confidence boost they all needed."

Andrew is genuinely impressed. "I'm beginning to understand your approach a lot better now. It seems that the fear-free feedback element of the training was a definite turning point for them."

"Definitely, and it's something I recommend you embed into the culture of your company."

There was silence for a few seconds while Andrew contemplated this. "So you're not recommending that I should get rid of any of the underperformers?"

"Andrew, you don't have any dead wood – not among the six people I trained, anyway. The only dead wood is that antiquated sales manual they were given during their induction. They just need encouragement, support and some fear-free feedback from you both." I look at Andrew and then at Adrienne.

Andrew turns to Adrienne. "What do you think?"

"I agree with Jamie's assessment," she says. "I've worked with him before and I've seen this transform a sales function in a business like ours."

Andrew sits back in his chair. "Okay, next steps. Is there a plan in place?"

Adrienne nods. "Yes, we've got plans that we're working on. That includes putting the rest of the sales team through this training programme, because everyone's dying to know what happened on the course with Jamie – there's a real buzz going around."

Andrew keeps his attention focused on Adrienne. "Have you seen a difference in the six who have been trained?"

"To be honest, I'm seeing a completely transformed team. It's only been a couple of weeks and the difference is really noticeable."

"Like what?"

"For example, the team have already responded to the training itself. They want to create their own sales toolkit using Jamie's methodology and have asked if there's a budget to create posters for the sales floor that show key learning points from the course. As a visual stimulus, that's going to help them tremendously."

"What about with the customers? Have you seen anything change?"

"Yes. I've been monitoring this closely. Statistically, the conversations are lasting longer and the team are spending a lot more time on discovery, which has gone through the roof. I'm hearing a lot more questions being asked of the customers."

"You're listening to the calls as well, then?"

"Yes. I can really hear them picking out the hooks for opportunities to sell in other parts of the call, which they weren't doing before Jamie's training. People like Ros and Naomi are also much more confident and yesterday I heard Ros reflecting to Naomi that she missed a great opportunity to link a benefit of a product to a specific interest the customer had."

"What did Naomi say?"

"She was really pleased Ros told her and said she would definitely remember that next time around. Before, they wouldn't have known how to do this. So far, we've only put six of the sales team through Jamie's training and already they're not getting as many dead leads, they're handling difficult calls much more effectively and we're seeing an increase in orders and a jump in our revenue. Think what could be achieved by rolling out the whole training programme to the rest of the sales team."

"You definitely forecast we can grow because of this?"

"Yes. Long term, I can see this having a huge impact on the plans and on our revenue, which means that we can deliver on what you need, Andrew."

Almost as if Andrew is struck by a bolt of lightning, he sits upright in his chair. "Right, we need to roll this out as soon as possible. I wish this had happened a year ago. Adrienne, I'm going to leave this with you – do what's needed to get the ball rolling. I want everyone to attend this training, okay?"

CHAPTER 6

THE IMPACT

Three months later, almost to the day, Adrienne is called into Andrew's office for a meeting to discuss the next quarter's sales projections.

Much has happened in the intervening period. I have been able to deliver a staggered programme of training sessions with the rest of FusionTech's sales force.

Over the last few weeks, the sales figures have noticeably improved and are exceeding the target increase of five per cent. As a result, Andrew has been able to think about bringing the business expansion plans forward.

The progress the business has achieved in such a short time has given Andrew a more buoyant air than usual. Impressed with how well Adrienne has performed and what she has delivered, he looks up from the report and offers his warm congratulations. "I didn't think you could pull this off."

Adrienne, confident in knowing that her plans have paid off and demonstrated her good judgement in bringing in Jamie, laughs and says, "Of course I could pull it off."

"Yes, but this is more than good work, Adrienne – this is exceptional. The projections for the next twenty-four months show we're really moving in the right direction, at last. It's good to know I'm not the only one driving everything round here, for once, and that I can rely on other people to deliver."

"That's why you hired me, isn't it?"

"It is, but you've achieved more in less than six months than others could in six years. Well done."

"Thanks, but I really can't take all the credit. Jamie's worked wonders here."

"I know. I admit, I was sceptical at first, probably a little offended by his claims that he could increase our margins by so much and so quickly, but he was as good as his word. Right now, we're ahead of target. In fact, I've got a kick-off meeting with the expansion-planning task force this afternoon."

"So, the ball is rolling," Adrienne smiles warmly. "Oh, and on another positive note, because we're converting more enquiries into sales, we're not spending so much on marketing."

Andrew nods. "Everyone seems to be pulling together and doing a brilliant job. Jamie was right when he said we didn't need to lose anybody."

"I know. I've seen a real difference, especially in cross-selling and up-selling. Actually, our consulting team are now getting to grips with their questioning techniques and spending longer with their customers. I've even heard that some are asking for salespeople by name," Adrienne leans forward as she speaks, as if confiding a secret.

"Take Steve, for example – customers seem to have really taken to him and he's anticipating their needs because of the questions he asks them. They're all working at a higher level than they were three months ago and delivering consistently."

"Do you think if we offered Jamie a job as our training director, he'd take it?" Andrew is serious.

Adrienne laughs. “He’d be flattered to be asked, I’m sure. But every company he works with offers him that after they start seeing the results he creates.”

“Well?”

“It’s not going to happen.”

“That’s ridiculous. Couldn’t we just make him an offer he can’t refuse? Who’d say no to that?”

“You can ask him if you like.”

“Well, why not? Why wouldn’t he want to?”

“Truth is, Andrew, we don’t need him. We’ve got what we need to get us to where we’re going with the expansion plans. Jamie has his own company and he’s always in demand. I doubt anything we could offer him would tempt him.”

“I thought you’d jump at the chance to work with him again.”

“Oh, I will be working with him again. Sooner rather than later, I expect.”

“What does that mean?” Andrew looks puzzled.

"What we need most now is a dedicated customer service team to handle the increase in our after-sales calls."

"How does that involve Jamie?" Andrew asks.

"It won't be long until we'll need him to train the new customer service team on how to *maintain* relationships with existing customers – not just *forge* relationships with new ones."

Andrew is silent for several seconds as he contemplates this idea. "Okay, that sounds like a good plan. Put a proposal and cost model together for me and we'll go over the figures."

Adrienne stands up and walks towards Andrew's office door. She spins round as Andrew adds.

"Oh, and call Jamie. Give him a heads up that we're gonna need him again for a brand new project."

"Will do." Adrienne smiles and heads for her phone.

To be continued…

CONCLUSION

Firstly, thank you for reading *Socially Intelligent Selling*. I hope you appreciated its fly-on-the-wall style and that you enjoyed a taste of what it's like to be in the training room with me.

I wanted you to gain an insight into how my methodology works in practice and discover for yourself the techniques that you can now try at your desk.

Each character I encountered during my time at FusionTech is purposely based on real individuals who I meet every day in my work at The Skills Farm. My aim was that one or more of them would resonate with you and seem familiar. If you did relate to Andrew, Adrienne or any of the workshop participants, you'll realise now that a shift in your thinking and approach is absolutely possible.

Throughout this book, I've laid out the self-awareness and interpersonal techniques that socially intelligent sales professionals use to make tangible and rewarding connections with their customers. Interestingly, many people I meet in the training room believe that they are already excellent communicators and have nothing to learn. This inability to judge accurately our own capacity to communicate is common. It takes an emotionally intelligent individual with a growth mindset to listen to subtle (or even not so subtle) feedback from their team, their managers and their customers.

As my training courses unfold, the trust among members of the sales team deepens. However, this is not inevitable. It takes a skilled and somewhat brave facilitator to ensure that individuals in the team are given the opportunity to show their vulnerability. When teammates admit to what they don't know, don't understand, or don't say or do, something interesting happens – the team galvanises and its members pull together and start supporting each other. The sooner an individual's defences are lowered, the quicker trust builds and the stronger the team becomes. Robust sales teams give and receive fear-free feedback.

My intention is that now you've read my book, you'll be willing to offer clear, timely, specific fear-free feedback to others on your team and to receive feedback just as fearlessly. This approach to willing, continuous improvement is one of the most effective ways to build excellence and consistency across the entire sales team – and it's available to everyone. Remember, nobody wins unless everybody wins.

As you saw at FusionTech, the socially intelligent sales team generated more revenue for the company and this caused a ripple effect across other departments. As well as making a measurable financial impact, people felt invested in so there was a positive impact on morale and motivation levels too.

Company management teams who think that it's enough to hand out a training manual or even send their people on a cheap, off-the-shelf training course are missing a trick. Training must be tailored to the specific needs of each company and fit the culture of the people who work there. Time must be spent getting to know what makes a company tick and what's preventing it from moving forward. Only then can a company hope to accurately measure the return on its training investment.

Talking of ripple effect, you might have noticed that I'm due to return to FusionTech to train their customer service team in my revolutionary customer relationship programme. Scott, my husband, is looking forward to getting his hands on the FusionTech management team and taking them through his approach to becoming a confident, inspiring leader. For that, you'll have to wait until books two and three.

For now, I'll leave you to contemplate the sales-turnover distress that FusionTech were in before I helped them turn their tired and traditional sales regime into a socially intelligent sales machine that is reaping real results.

More importantly, perhaps you can now see why your own organisation is suffering sales stagnation and how a bespoke training programme that works can transform your business into the success it deserves to be.

Remember, training shouldn't be the same old repetitive tick-box process that's dull, boring and ineffective. Training should be stimulating, challenging, revealing and highly engaging. It must also be shown to impact the bottom line and provide a company with opportunities to grow.

When your sales team are trained to be socially intelligent, they become a winning team – and when they win, everyone wins.

SOCIALLY INTELLIGENT SELLING WORKSHOP

Ready to apply what you've read here?

Jamie and his team run two-day workshops on socially intelligent selling in organisations up and down the country every year. He provides a safe environment for intensive learning, practice and feedback proven to increase sales, conversion rates and revenue.

So, if you're truly determined to become a socially intelligent salesperson or team and you're ready to reap the rewards, email sociallyintelligentselling@theskillsfarm.co.uk to find out more.

ACKNOWLEDGEMENTS

It may be my name on the front of this book, but the credit for making it happen has to go to five key people.

Firstly, my wonderful husband, Scott Summers. Without you the words in this book would still be sitting inside my head. Thank you for helping me overcome my fear of writing and for guiding every word out of me and onto the paper.

Secondly, Peter Mitchell. With your trust in me and generous investment, the ideas and techniques in this book can now be shared around the world. Thank you.

Thirdly, Lucy McCarraher and Mike Elliston. Thank you for patience, kindness and understanding. Over three years your support has been invaluable in helping me write a book despite my dyslexia.

And finally, Christa Gould. Thank you for believing in me all those years ago and pushing me into a sales role.

Had you not spotted my ability to sell socially, this book may have been about being a world-class receptionist instead.

THE AUTHOR

Jamie Summers is an award-winning trainer and co-founder of The Skills Farm.

In 2002, at age twenty-four, Jamie landed his first sales role at an estate agent in Manchester, England. He was quickly recognised as having a special touch with clients and within a year of working there he had written his first training workshop, How to Take Our Customers on a Journey.

This pattern repeated throughout his career. In each sales role he accepted, Jamie would soon be asked to train his team members on how to sell like he did.

By the age of thirty-three Jamie was training and coaching store staff at Apple Retail in London on how to become socially intelligent at selling and uncover sales opportunities through natural conversations. In 2013 he won the Apple Spirit of Business award for his work.

Jamie and his husband Scott – at the time an award-winning, experienced leadership skills trainer at IBM – joined forces and created The Skills Farm. Together, using Jamie's socially intelligent selling methodology they won work with clients such as Google, Deloitte and the NHS.

Today, Jamie is regularly asked to speak at events around the country. Specifically, he is known for transforming the fortunes of sales teams across a variety of industries. His unique and approachable style is highly regarded by leadership teams and participants alike. As a result, his training workshops are fully booked months in advance.

You can contact Jamie at:

Web: www.theskillsfarm.co.uk
Email: jamiesummers@theskillsfarm.co.uk
Twitter: @theskillsfarm
LinkedIn: linkedin.com/in/jamiewsummers

57386708R00099

Made in the USA
Middletown, DE
30 July 2019